Take My Advice & Please Yourself

after all, I may be a raving
psychotic lunatic
(but I'm probably not)

A Portrait of a Modern-Day
Spiritual Initiate

By Some of His Students

To order more copies or to contact the authors
visit: wwww.vividpublishing.com.au/theinsightseries

Copyright © 2025 Students of Michael King
ISBN: 978-1-923078-59-8

Published by Vivid Publishing
A division of Fontaine Publishing Group
P.O. Box 948, Fremantle
Western Australia 6959
www.vividpublishing.com.au

A catalogue record for this book is available from the National Library of Australia

All rights reserved. No part of this publication may be reproduced, stored in a retrieval system or transmitted in any form or by any means, electronic, mechanical, photocopying, recording or otherwise, without the prior written permission of the copyright holder.

*In honour of our teacher, mentor,
way-shower, light-bearer and friend,
Michael.*

*Using our words as brushstrokes,
we attempt to paint your portrait
on behalf of all those
whose lives you have changed,
and to instil hope
in those who may still be seeking.*

CONTENTS

~~~

Introduction	1
Story One	15
Story Two	29
Story Three	44
Story Four	65
Story Five	76
Story Six	89
Story Seven	107
Story Eight	116
Story Nine	130
Story Ten	140
Story Eleven	147
Story Twelve	167
Story Thirteen	186
Afterword	200
What Next?	205

Introduction

~ ~ ~

"The journey of a thousand miles begins with a single step."
- Lao Tzu

We, a small but diverse group of Michael's students, felt inspired to compile this book on the most evolved being I have encountered in this life, in an attempt to ignite hope and to remind the world that extraordinary people such as Michael do still exist, and though they are very few in numbers, they walk amongst us, hidden to all except those whose hearts are ready to recognise, and those whose eyes are ready to see.

Personally, I could write a rather large library on this subject, not because I'm a prolific writer, but because Michael is an inexhaustible wealth of Wisdom and Knowing (the voice of our heart), so incredibly articulate and able to discourse in detail on just about anything.

We aspire to convey the experience of working with a great soul. The work is grounded, real and different to anything I had previously engaged in or envisaged. It's not about angels, dolphins, fluffy bunnies and rainbows. If this is what you seek, then you may perhaps fall into the category of being a bit of a space cadet. If you are also inclined to incessant thinking and using your mind inappropriately, then perhaps you are more of a head-tripping space cadet.

Either way, to work with Michael is to come down out of the clouds, and to find yourself, instead, fully present and actively serving, here on planet earth. Rather than training up spiritual pontificators, well-versed in theory and presumption, Michael focuses on training up what can most accurately be described as spiritual warriors who are actively perceiving of, and responding to, divine plan and intention – ones who are attempting to embody and exemplify higher truths through their lived, witnessed, and felt human lives.

Contrary to what most people on the spiritual path are led to believe, there are few beings such as Michael walking on the planet in these moments. It is a precious, priceless opportunity and something that needs to be respected, cherished, and held in the sacredness that it deserves and requires.

It is most likely that the opportunity to learn from one such as Michael won't come at all if we don't prepare ourselves earnestly. We don't get to learn from these beings because we are willing to pay a lot of money for the privilege, and no number of weekend workshops will bring about the substantial and long-lasting evolutionary transformations that any true seeker yearns for, no matter how much money was spent. These transformations must be worked for, and they come about naturally when the student becomes ready. No one can initiate you – no one is able to override free will and evolution in this way. Initiation is the natural by-product of adequate preparation, activation, and actualisation. Never did this adage apply more, "when the student is ready, the teacher appears".

It is not us who chooses the Initiate that we study with, or the service we are called to fulfil as part of our purpose for being here. We are called and attracted to an Initiate and a service project based on our strengths, abilities, skills, history, and past service records over many lifetimes. Each Initiate, although similar in fundamental ways, is different in expression and each has particular specialities and projects which they work with.

In the end, it's not about "me", "myself" and "I". It is about what we can contribute and offer up in service of the divine plan. This intention must be strong in our heart and our understanding. If we are still focusing a lot of life energy and activity in an attempt to foster our own happiness, then we are a long way off. In the end, everything becomes about what we can give back, how we may serve, what we can bring to the planet, how we can facilitate the nurturance of all life, and the part we can play in something grander and more far-reaching than just ourselves.

When we find and recognise our path, our heart will be touched as our soul remembers. We will be moved on a feeling level by the teachings, energy and people involved. Rather than being about pleasing our lower self or our fear-based ego, this kind of recognition calls to our heart and soul. Transformation does not happen by thinking or reading about it, or by observing from a distance. We must involve ourselves and allow ourselves to be moved.

Such is the absence of heart purity and clarity, that even those who are called to this path can be oblivious, trip over such an opportunity, and then walk right on past as if nothing had happened. Or perhaps those who are called might have a strong ego and use the incoming energy to activate their negative ego (the part of the ego which is charged with fear) to such a degree that delusion knocks them out of the ring. Alas, the first step on the path is recognition, and the first task is to transmute and refine the ego so that negative ego strength is minimal.

We are living in a world that is full of people who are trapped in the limiting imprisonment of three-dimensional thraldom, trying desperately to preserve themselves in the fear that is rampant. The kingdom of humanity is so prone to living life through the lens of an ego, behaving as a life support for this miniscule aspect of the totality of our being, thinking that we are being very spiritual and not really experiencing spirituality at all.

This phenomenon can make it challenging for budding initiates to rise out of the quagmire. Humans are getting tangled up in the illusion, glamour and maya that is prevalent, distorting the truth and letting true liberation slip through their fingertips. I almost fell into this trap and nearly missed my opportunity to work with Michael.

Upon reading these pages, you may get a sense of what is required to be ready for such an opportunity and you may be inspired to put the hard work into preparing yourself accordingly, so that when you are called, you are able to take full advantage and not miss the cosmic bus. Or, if you have already found your spiritual home, make the most of the golden opportunity. The new age community has been corrupted to a large degree and there is a lot of gobbledygook out there about what it means to be spiritual, so one must tread carefully and be discerning.

If you are looking for someone to teach you magical tricks and psychic skills that can only ever serve to puff up your ego, then this is not the path, or the book, for you. Michael would say, 'Only ever exert energy if it is going to ground and express more love. If it's not about grounding and expressing more love, then it's just art for art's sake.' He would only ever expend energy in the service of love.

This book is not intended to be a spiritual jacuzzi where we bliss out in the higher light bodies togther. It's a wakeup call that you may find sobering if you have been hearing this clarion call and ignoring it, or if you have been getting tangled up in spiritual activities that will not produce the desired results.

We all came into this life with gifts and skills from previous lives, which will come on board organically when we make ourselves a safe host and clear channel for spirit.

We do this by gaining mastery over our four-body system; physically, emotionally, mentally and at primal soul level. The area which is the most unclear in humans in these moments, and which needs the most work, is clearing ourselves psychologically. If we force our gifts to come on board without doing the hard yards of gaining psychological clarity, we can do damage. Some examples of the shortcuts people try to take are spinning Merkabah's, taking drugs, and advanced breathing techniques to force the kundalini to rise.

Evolution and activation must unfold gradually, and in divine timing. The bodies must be properly prepared and made ready to house higher frequencies of energy. Taking shortcuts and blowing the veils open to forcefully partake of energy is bound to result in any number of a plethora of spiritual diseases, including schisms, a lack of integration, and literal death as the systems of the body become overloaded and blown out. The process of spiritual transformation is a thorough and holistic one, and it must be approached as such. If you are ready, then it will happen of its own accord. No one can make you ready, and no one can initiate something within you which you are not ready for.

Michael shared, 'Lightworkers are basically Universal immune cells that have been sent by the Universe to restore harmony to our beloved planet. Only around two percent of the lightworkers who were sent here have activated in these moments, either because they fell or because they got tangled up in hedonism, power, prestige and profit, so we are very short of help on the ground. It's no more complicated than that.'

There are many temptations in this day and age, and so few are willing to put in the hard work to actually be of service.

On the property he lived on and worked from, Michael constructed a war memorial-style monument, in memory of the lightworker heroes throughout time who have sacrificed their lives in service. On the plaque it read, "In Grateful Recognition of those selfless souls, who heroically live their lives as Champions of Enlightenment, of Love, and of Wisdom in Service to the Highest Potential of all concerned. May Love Restore the Balance." It was a very moving experience to be with this memorial and pay respects to our fallen comrades.

You may have that nagging feeling that you are off track, not where you are supposed to be. Perhaps you feel an emptiness within that you have tried to fill up with all manner of distractions that this world has to offer, yet each new thing that you try only makes the gaping hole within expand even more, with each failed attempt to return to wholeness.

Keep reading to find some assistance in detecting and recognising the many false prophets you may come across in your quest to become spirit identified and fit yourself for service. Without being paranoid, this kind of discernment will render you more able to attract an authentic teacher and to be in alignment with the highest good of all concerned, allowing life to suck you into place, so that you may fulfil your purpose here now.

There is a saying that "to be a master you have to know a master", and Michael has extended himself most generously, going to great lengths to impart in-depth experience and share his life as a soul journeying through eternity.

'Serious dedicated application, constancy and consistency, is required. In order to be successful, you need to want self-mastery more than you want to breathe, and your entire life needs to spin out of this central hub.'

If you fancy the idea of flying solo, you may want to think again. The accelerated ascension path is a group initiative, so no one can do it alone. This is obvious when we consider that once we expand out to the fifth dimension, there is no separation; we are all one, a mere droplet in an ocean of energy.

Nobody has ever completed planetary ascension and gotten through this system without receiving mentoring from someone who is a couple of steps ahead of them. There are many obstacles and there is much counter-intention, resistance and inertia pushing against us, attempting to keep us locked into the confines of humanity's collective evolutionary average.

Furthermore, once you find yourself a couple of steps ahead, it becomes imperative that you step into your role as an elder brother or sister of the race, lighting the way and assisting ones who are a couple of steps behind you.

This is how evolution occurs. By empowering another, assisting them to heal and grow, you are also assisting yourself, encouraging your own evolution forward as you make yourself useful and as you seek out new ways to remain useful. But, once your life has been given over to service, an over-emphasis on your own progress, your own evolution, and your own ascension has naturally been replaced by a love for humanity, and a yearning to serve and uplift in any way that you can. So, you offer assistance not for your own personal gain, but for the sake of nurturing all life, recognising that the same life force which flows through you, flows through all things.

If you are looking for a weekend hobby or a recreational pastime, where you get some tools that will assist you to rise out of the swamp of issues that you wish to avoid feeling through, then the accelerated ascension path is not something that you will be fit for. To be seriously on the path, we need to earnestly apply the three rules of spiritual success, which are to accept the unchangeable, change the changeable, and remove ourselves from the unacceptable.

Our motivations for seeking spiritual evolution need not be altruistic from the start – they will be tweaked and refined as we progress, with all selfish motivations eventually being replaced by selfless ones. If our only reason for initially stepping upon the path is that we simply can't stand our lives anymore, then this will produce minimum pass marks at best. Yet, this is a start, and all must start from exactly where they are at. Minimum pass marks can be improved upon. The important thing is that serious study has begun, and that there is an impetus to seek out and embrace change.

Once steady footing upon this new path has been established, one must get to work, diligently clearing all that stands in the way of selfless service, so that the motivation for being on the path is purely to ground and express more love.

I would recommend that you take your head off and let it rest on the nearby couch, as you won't need it for this experience. We use our minds way too much, employing them to conduct things that they were not designed for. The way to approach working with this book is by feeling your way through and allowing the feeling to move you and take you on a journey, a fully present involvement of feeling.

I've learnt a lot from my mistakes. There were some teachings that I, the ego, decided didn't apply to me. I was picking and choosing, and it wasn't until some years down the track that I realised my folly. The foundational principles are vital, for if we don't have strong foundations, we don't have a stable base to build upon when we expand, and our growth can quickly come tumbling down. The higher you go, the harder the fall.

The foundational principles must be visited and refined, again and again, to offset such tumbles – before reaching further, we must ensure that we are stable, steady, integrated, and present. If we are wavering, loose, ungrounded and unintegrated, then a sudden inpouring of more energy can only destabilise us. Inevitably, the cracks in the foundations will give, and the entire structure will buckle.

This lack of preparation and synthesis causes a great many aspiring initiates to fall. You cannot grow large and far-reaching branches without a solid, stable trunk and a sturdy, deeply penetrating root system. The beauty, vitality, grandeur and lifespan of the tree is dependent upon, and directly reflective of, the health of the underground support system – the foundations. For as much of the tree which is seen, there is as much which is unseen; quietly building, reaching and sustaining beneath the soil.

Michael never teaches quick fixes or encourages unwarranted or ungrounded highs – he feeds, waters and nurtures saplings which will grow to become great and ancient oaks; long-standing, teaching through their example, and providing shade and mulch for the entire forest for many years to come. He is thorough and steady in his approach, but the results are permanent as the changes occur in the root system – at the level of the soul – and slowly but surely translate to the rest of the tree – the physical, emotional and mental bodies.

Michael has shared that, 'The branch of alchemy that underpins this work is Personal Spiritual Alchemy. The more spiritual, metaphysical side of alchemy, continuing the search for immortality and the transmutation of base human nature into its highest potential (transforming and transmuting fear into love), to allow the fusion of the human being with its spiritual Source. To become spirit in human form, there are three basic stages:

The first one is to know thyself. This is the preparatory stage when the alchemist must confront unknown, chaotic material within themselves, to encounter the unillumined aspects within and enlighten them.

The second one is the transcension of duality within oneself. By imposing transcendent norms upon seemingly opposing polarities, one learns to master the nature of reality as simply an infinite scale of vibrational expression from infinity to unity.

The third one is the systematic investigation into one's own cosmic origins and the subsequent "revelation of Source".

Alchemy is alive and well in all its forms and expressions. One day soon we will all realise this, and it will be a great unifying revelation for the planet. It will lead to a new intensity of combined effort towards the betterment of humanity. In the final analysis, if you are serious about Personal Spiritual Alchemy, find someone a few steps ahead of you on that path and take instruction!'

When a group of initiates come together for a common purpose, it can be a magical, heart-cracking-open experience, something I'd not experienced in this life. When Michael was present, this was greatly amplified. We could sit around the table laughing and beaming with each other for hours, without alcohol or drugs. Part of this magical experience also included us providing the starkest mirrors and reflections for each other.

After some number of lives as the lone wolf in the wilderness (which had taken me far and wide in my travels and which had left me tangled up in pursuits that had little to do with my eternal wellbeing), when I found Michael, I knew that I had found my real home. I had finally found my true family, the purpose for my incarnation and existence, taking my place alongside other souls that I have journeyed with through many lifetimes.

Michael's discourses are multi-dimensional, entertaining, often humorous, and, when the tough love hammer is wielded as a means of cracking into otherwise unobtainable pockets of stuck energy, sometimes sobering. His teachings are always imparting a higher wisdom and helpful tips for working towards mastery. They are always offered with kindness and love. Michael is relentlessly finding new ways to say the same thing in as many different ways as possible, from as many angles and perspectives as possible, so that we might get it, whoever we are, wherever we're at, wherever we've come from, and wherever we're headed.

His teachings are multi-layered; they can be received at their most basic level, or they can be followed all the way through to the nucleus, to the Source energy which lies within. He holds his own energy in such a way that he offers himself up as an agent of evolution, allowing life itself to flow and express through him. This means that everything that he does and says leaves everyone feeling as though it were perfectly tailored to them – everyone gets what they need from him, all at once.

Michael works tirelessly to expose egoic behaviour so that it can be transcended. Everyone is treated according to what they need in the moment, and in the way which is most likely to produce an outcome of love. When Michael is facilitating, there is much going on in the unseen and feelings levels, and it is important to be open to receiving spiritual transmissions, rather than getting caught up in grasping at ideas with the intellect.

The teacher never does anything that the student can do, so as soon as a student is ready, Michael passes on tasks. This is always a stretch and an opportunity for the student to grow, and it allows the teacher to step into new roles. One doesn't leave one's station until they have found a replacement, and Michael often shares that his goal is to make himself redundant – far from wanting to be special or to be the best, he is interested in producing competent Initiates who can do what he does, and more.

Michael's wife and business partner, Segolene, a great soul in her own right, explained the mechanism of how the process works:

'It is a path of spiritual growth and heart mastery which is different to traditional religious paths, Western or Eastern. The religious path to spiritual development relies on the mechanism of devotion to someone who represents an intermediary between yourself and God/Source.

This path relies on the mechanism of Insight and Self-Mastery, thereby removing the long-term need for an intermediary between yourself and Source. It works in a way which energetically holds you in spiritual energies of unconditional love and above and mirrors your own soul's reflection to yourself.

When you are receptive, this can assist you to realise, acknowledge, feel and release the various aspects of ego, fear and self-imposed limitation which you carry from this life and others. We call this process "psychological clearing". The same reflective mechanism will also reflect your greater potential, in order to inspire you to stretch yourself beyond your current comfort zones, and therefore grow.

We teach Integrated Self-Mastery. This means that we are not keen on being spacey, floating in "fluffy love" land, disconnected from the world around us and even from our own humanity and its struggles. We seek to bring greater Love, Light and Truth where it is most needed, here on earth, in the world of humans and other creatures, and into all our experience. For this to be possible, we must remain grounded, present, in humility and willing to courageously love the unlovable, thereby bringing Love and Light into dark and disconnected places. We seek to not only be loving, but powerfully loving, as part of our service.'

When I met Michael, he didn't fit into the stereotyped spiritual teacher box that I had conjured up, and I rejoiced. One of Michael's favourite sayings is, 'What people think of me is none of my business'. That's not to say that Michael won't listen to what others have to say – there is no arrogance or self-righteousness in his approach, and he is always open to self-reflection – but he doesn't seek approval from others. He simply compares himself with his own potential, and strives, in every moment, to embody more of the ideal that he senses.

The content of this book has come from our personal contact with Michael, be it at social events, or through attending weekly classes and retreats over a period of time. Our identities are not relevant to the task at hand, and so we have chosen to remain anonymous, focusing instead upon our stories of our teacher. We offer ourselves as a lens and as a mouthpiece, but rather than focusing on us, we encourage you to focus inward. Our recognition and our experiences may point to a deeper truth and understanding which lies within you.

When we refer to fear, we are referring to any feeling which is not love, such as anger, sadness, guilt, hurt, resentment, desolation, hopelessness, apathy. By the same token, there are many different expressions of love, such as discernment, calm assurance, hope, optimism, compassion, clarity, awareness, truth, grace.

Any serious Initiate is able to express love in a multitude of ways – there are as many ways to love as there are individuals, feelings, experiences, and circumstances. We have attempted to share, throughout this book, the many different ways that Michael expresses his love. You will notice, if you are allowing yourself to feel, that each of Michael's students is unique – that each experiences Michael in a way which is specific to them, that each recognises and partakes of a frequency of his love which best serves and uplifts them. Let yourself experience the full plethora and bandwidth of love which is being shared with you, recognising those frequencies which resonate with you, rattling your heart free of the confines of your own fear and contraction.

As you read, keep in mind that each one of us has walked a unique path, and that each one of us approaches life and our spiritual path in a unique way. Be sure to greet each of us, his students, anew, bringing no expectations or preconceived ideas – it is important to remember that neither the age of the physical body nor the amount of time spent working with Michael is indicative of the age of the soul. Each one of us is at different stages in our evolution, overcoming particular shortcomings and realising specific potentials. We are not perfect, and never would we claim to be. But we have, perhaps, been where you are now, and we hope that, by sharing a little bit of what has helped us along the way, we can now offer you some perspective and assistance. Be in discernment, but remember to receive us as we are, just as we will aim to receive you and embrace you as you are.

Feel and partake of our experiences of our great teacher and allow his love to reach through us as you see him through our eyes, hear him through our ears, and receive him through our hearts. Though you may not personally know Michael, his love is such that you will feel and receive it in a way which is perfectly tailored to you, your experience, your requirements, and your potential. With your boundaries set at unconditional love and above, drink freely and deeply of the profound and immensely transformative energy of one who can greet you, receive you, know you and love you, exactly as you are.

Receive, and allow yourself to be received in return.

STORY ONE

~ ~ ~

I had a very deep and profound experience of recognition upon first meeting Michael. Well, just prior to meeting him in person. It was at a time when I was feeling very lost and broken. I felt so far from my life's calling and so far from the experience of my rich inner reality seeping through to the outer. The only true connection I felt to the outer world was when I was in nature. I recognised nature as being the outer expression of the divine. Prior to meeting Michael, I pretty much hid on the inner – the higher dimensional planes seemed more real to me, and my human life felt like the dream that I could not wait to wake up from, so keen was I to be back on the inner. Here is a glimpse of how profoundly not present, out of balance and ungrounded I initially was.

Rather than identifying with my body, my experience was more like viewing my embodiment. Most of my early life was lived in third person. My first true awareness was when I received my first instruction as a child. The message was clear – I was to 'Find Michael'. This instruction resounded within me and was always with me and as I grew. I met so many Michaels along the way, and although I didn't understand why finding Michael was so important, I knew that none of the Michaels I met were the Michael that I was searching for.

In my late teens I married a Michael, even though I sensed he was not the one. That truth was profoundly and clearly communicated to me by the sinking feeling in my heart as I walked down the aisle toward a future that was taking me further away from my inner calling. As a result of not being present in my life, I let myself be buffeted about and drawn into other people's realities. I felt a powerlessness and an inability to grip my own life. There was a lot of messy history between me and my husband, a strong karmic pull and a rich past which needed to be cleared, released and harmonised. For this reason, my first marriage was difficult and tumultuous.

Some years later, I found myself in my second marriage, feeling even further off track. For some time, I had been reaching out to upstairs, to my inner plane friends and guides, saying, 'please help me, I am so lost'. I felt so broken and hopeless and like I was living a lie, and now I was putting out a desperate call for some direction, or for a sign.

The profound yet quiet moment that completely changed the direction of my life happened in 1998. I was going about my usual daily things when a rush of energy and a feeling of deep connection suddenly came over me. Something, a remembering, was waking up inside of me. My inner world became so illuminated, and I could feel Michael in my awareness. I knew that he was physically close, and I knew that I would see him soon. I looked the same on the outside, but my experience was dramatically changing. Something far greater than my small human reality was taking me over.

My inner vision and my rich inner awareness were opening here in my person. Visual and intuitive gifts and abilities were switching on. Even though they had always been a part of my rich inner reality, it felt like they were "here" for the first time. My rich inner reality was coming to life in a new and deeper way, here, and I could see the matrix. I could see Michael. Not in a physical way – I saw him energetically, I felt him, I remembered him, I recognised him. His energy signature was here in my heart and an experience of timelessness washed over me in this remembering and recognition.

I was consciously aware of immediately joining Michael's inner plane classes – these are ascension classes which Michael, as a soul, energetically facilitates on higher planes. A lot of my initial training was on the inner as I went through the healing, clearing and grounding which was necessary to become more present, so that I could really come into my body and embrace my life on the ground.

At the time of this experience, Michael was on the edge of the small Queensland town I lived in, heading to our place with a friend of my husbands at the time, who was coming to see about some paint. I could fill a whole book with the details of that first meeting with Michael, but I will sum it up by saying that it was profound and other worldly, whilst also being quiet but inwardly exuberant. He was so accepting and loving. It was like meeting an old friend and having a deep sense of coming home. How simple and magical life can be when all is not what it seems. My healing and training with a teacher began right then and there, and the journey continues as it began.

After meeting Michael, my life changed dramatically, and I was so grateful. I had been asking and now I was receiving. Even as each step felt so right and the knowing was so strong, I felt guided by a greater and deeper part of myself whom I felt to naturally embrace. It was me; it wasn't anything outside of me. It felt like a greater or a new and more expanded part of me was taking me in this new direction, following my hearts guidance and answering my soul's service calling. At the same time as everything was changing, I felt a deep sense of familiarity. Rather than being taken away from myself, I was having the experience of coming more into myself – of recognising and coming home to more of myself.

This awakening was certainly not without its challenges, and, at times, I encountered incredible resistance from my own negative ego, and from my family and the people around me. I took the steps quite quickly. I made changes very rapidly. I knew I needed to ride the wave of this awakening and keep up with the momentum, taking action in what felt like right timing. With no time for thinking or doubting (though I did have moments of that), and with an intense awareness of just how quickly things can turn into missed opportunities, I turned my life around.

This is where I first experienced "windows opening" and "windows closing". Without energy or the right kind of focus, some things may simply not be able to happen. Opportunities must be embraced in right timing. Instead of being influenced by the "ticks of a clock" or by the thoughts or opinions of others or by our own fears and insecurities, we must learn to be guided and inspired by the divine timing which orchestrates windows of opportunity.

I had already made my choice, and by making this choice, I had set energy in motion. By utilising my free will, I had created an energetic momentum which was seeking to move me forward. I felt as though I had been chosen for something, and now I also needed to choose myself. I needed to let go and to release myself into the flow of the energy and the focused guidance which encouraged me.

Through this experience, I began to understand how we are all creating our own reality – we are all, always, choosing. We are all, always, setting energy in motion. Life is always responding to our energetic output, diligently delivering us those things which we focus upon. I realised that, by focusing on negative things, I was outputting my energy in such a way that I was creating negative experiences for myself. I also realised that, rather than choosing to create suffering and pain for myself, I could choose to create growth and transformation and upliftment and joy.

I decided that I was going to start working with energy in a more conscious and deliberate kind of way. I decided that I wanted to be an active participant in my life, working to create outcomes of love. I also realised just how important it was that I became fully grounded and present in my life, taking the role of a facilitator rather than a spectator. I recognised this presence in Michael – through his unwavering stillness and his robust involvement in life, this was something that he very simply and naturally embodied and demonstrated for me, encouraging me and showing me how I could do the same.

Since meeting Michael and joining his inner plane classes, my inner communion with him had felt very strong and constant. At the time, my own fear and my own insecurities caused me to be too reserved and reluctant to approach Michael more directly on the ground, but one day I plucked up the courage and called him on the phone. This ended up being a simple phone conversation which was profound and, again, life changing.

I shared with Michael about my family and the people around me, their thoughts and opinions of me, and how it was difficult and draining. Michael strongly and simply said, 'Well that's none of your business, absolutely none of your business. What they think and feel is their own business, so why would it have anything to do with you?'. I was quite shocked in a good way. This rocked me. His response was very unexpected, and I felt such a freedom in releasing my family's thoughts and opinions of me as I realised that their thoughts and opinions were about them, not about me. I felt a weight lift from me, a lightness and a freedom came over me.

How wonderful and brilliant, my first insights into no longer taking things personally. This resulted in my setting stronger, clearer, more self-loving and self-respecting boundaries. I realised that setting boundaries was not a selfish thing to do. In fact, I realised that by loving and respecting myself more, I was also able to love and respect other people more. Rather than projecting my own thoughts and opinions outwards, I was now able to simply allow others to have their own experience. Who was I to meddle? Each individual is on their own unique journey of evolution. Each person has things to learn, things to realise, things to contend with, things to overcome. If I wanted other people to respect my reality and my right to make my own decisions, then surely, I must do the same for them. This is simply good energetic manners.

During this phone call, Michael also shared with me about cords and energetic connections. He explained to me the importance of clearing and cleansing and releasing these cords and connections, so that I was not so deeply impacted by other people and their energy. Rather than being an energetic doormat, receiving the brunt of other people's projections and giving them free access to my own energy, Michael taught me how to release all energy which was not of me, lovingly sending it back to its original source. I feel this was the greatest gift and this simple energetic hygiene process is one of our most important foundational healing and clearing tools, enabling us to truly be able to "know thyself".

Years later, I found myself, for the first time, suddenly grounding and landing in my body. After being absent for so long, suddenly finding myself being present was a bit of a shock. Finally, I could feel myself exactly as I was, and I felt annihilated. I felt very unwell. I was in touch, for the first time ever, with the effects of a long-term eating disorder which I'd had since my teenage years. I was in shock at how rejected and neglected I felt, and at how sick I was. I felt like a mess. I felt hopeless and so far away from my rich inner reality and any kind of composure in my person.

At the peak of this experience, Michael was facilitating an in-person class. The last thing I felt like doing was attending a class, but at the same time, I really loved and valued the process, the teachings and the work, and there was no way I was going to miss a class. My commitment was stronger than my resistance, and so I gathered myself up and went along.

I felt so small and decided to slip in and sit right in the back row. I was present, but I was also hiding myself away and I was feeling so far from wanting any attention or interactions with anyone. Of course, Michael noticed this.

Michael opened the class. Everyone settled in, and then his focus went straight to me as he said, 'I think May* is attempting to hide down the back there'. I was now entering my worst nightmare. He continued, 'She's been going through a big process and getting in touch with patterns of avoidance and denial, and now she's getting in touch with more of the truth of her experience'.

Then came a mortifying moment – a moment which would have previously resulted in me withdrawing into the depths of myself, becoming locked up in my own fear and my own self-defeating patterns and trauma responses (as I had done for much of my life). Michael continued, 'May would like to come up the front here and share with us her experience of the process she is undergoing.' Oh my God. Most of me wanted to run out of the room and straight for the hills. It took every ounce of any will I could muster to stand up, to stay in myself and face this crippling fear, and to walk the full length of the room to Michael.

* *name has been changed*

Feeling what I thought were the burning stares of a full class of people, it felt like the worst moment of my life. It seemed to take so long to get to the front of the class, and I had never been so uncomfortable or felt so exposed. I was feeling such intense judgement. I don't know what part of me was taking me to the front of the class when most of me wanted to run in the other direction, but I'm glad that I didn't run.

I felt Michael loving me and he greeted me as if I was not a broken and pathetic mess. He greeted me as if I was loved and as if I was accepted, exactly as I was. He greeted me as if what I was going through was perfectly okay. This was the strangest feeling. It was directly confronting and opposing, blowing out the water of these perceived "truths" that I carried within me, disproving my belief that I was horrible and pathetic and so deeply unlovable.

This became a new and tangible experience for me – it was proof that I was, in fact, lovable. Michael was loving me while I was spiralling in my belief that I had nothing to offer, feeling my absolute worst with a whole classroom full of people who were looking at me. I felt so mortified by what they must be thinking. I did feel like I was going to fall down

Michael put a chair out for me, right there in front of the class, and in that moment, I was completely giving over to the situation because there was nowhere to go and nowhere to hide. I looked around the room at the faces staring back at me, and I can't remember now what I said. I know I did not say very much, and I know it perhaps didn't even make sense. Michael also spoke, and I remember that what he was saying was loving and supportive and encouraging.

As I allowed myself to be there, I realised that there was no judgment coming from the other people in the room – instead, what I felt from them was a gentle kindness. I felt their curiosity and I felt a generosity which extended to include me as if I belonged there. I realised, in that moment, that the intense judgement I was feeling was not from the people, it was my own. But no matter how intense my judgement was, it was no match for the love and the acceptance I was being held in, and it quickly dissipated.

This was incredibly healing; it was one of my first profound healing experiences. To be so paralysed with fear, so full of my own judgement and self-loathing, and to walk what initially felt like "the plank" with sharks circling beneath, only to have such a new experience of being held and loved and accepted, was deeply and profoundly moving. This experience changed me, and I felt freed somehow – those deeply held beliefs were not true and I felt this ripple right through me.

At the same time as I was feeling very raw and exposed, I also felt an authentic presence in being vulnerable, and I experienced the healing power of being held in acceptance and unconditional love. My life felt like it was in my hands, and I felt that nothing could be done to me that I did not choose or allow.

I went back to my seat feeling profoundly changed and incredibly grateful to Michael. I don't know how else I could have learned this lesson and experienced this healing.

Often, our greatest healing comes, and our most significant lessons are learned, from facing and overcoming our greatest fears. Michael understands this. Out of a deep love for all of his students, Michael seeks to safely facilitate processes which will enable us to move beyond self-limiting beliefs and confines. With our evolution at the fore, he encourages us to courageously move forward, loving us, guiding us, and supporting us every step of the way. Every challenge is perfectly orchestrated to facilitate realisation and transformation.

From the moment that I met Michael, I witnessed him being a masterful example of his teaching. Once, when I was visiting him at his home, I found Michael in the living room. I went in and greeted him. At this time, I was still very reserved and timid. He got up from his chair and started moving about the room, acting very strangely. In my deepening observation of him, I wondered if he was okay. He was being a little dramatic, sighing deeply, and acting restless and unsettled.

After a time, he dropped himself back down in his chair and said, 'I'm so pathetic, I hate myself', and he went on like this for a time. I was a bit shocked. Why was he behaving like this? Surely, he wouldn't hate himself. I was quite concerned, and in observing him more closely it suddenly dawned on me: oh my God, this is not him, he is reflecting me – he is playing out how I am.

I wasn't in touch with it, until suddenly it became obvious and somewhat embarrassing. It was quite a sobering experience, and it was a little confronting to see myself so blatantly. When I finally understood the reflection, he had a slight smile, and compassionately, without any words about it, he continued on as himself. It was such an eye opener and such a masterful demonstration of the many and mysterious ways that an initiate can work with his students.

So smoothly and selflessly, Michael offers his students the reflections that they need. Deep self-introspection is not enough on its own, and sometimes being told a thing outright is likely to trigger a defensive reaction which causes the message to become distorted or completely dismissed. It is so easy to miss things, and the correct approach must be chosen for each unique individual and situation. Time and again, I have witnessed Michael surrender his body to become a perfectly clear mirror for his students, reflecting their countenance, their outlook, their beliefs, their pain and their limitations back to them in a tangible and undeniable way – 'here, this is what you are doing and here, this is what it looks like'. This is inevitably followed by a swift change in countenance and demeanour which demonstrates, 'here, this is what you could do instead; this is how you overcome this particular dilemma'. More important to him than what others think of him is his ability to assist others in their insight, growth and transformation.

In a way which transcends any kind of deception or dishonesty, Michael will bring himself to life and to people in the way which is most likely to produce an outcome of love. It matters not how he feels – Michael has a prior commitment to love which he upholds in all moments, teaching and demonstrating this love in whatever way he can.

The world is our mirror; it reflects our own internal state of being. If you want to change the mirror, you must change the energetic output which causes the mirror to reflect in a certain way. Outer change comes from within.

On several occasions, I have experienced Michael out in public, relating with strangers in a way which I have found to be just brilliant and quite beautiful. On these occasions, I would always feel my heart smiling warmly for the people who interacted with him. No matter how simple or brief the interaction, I knew that, on some level, their lives would not be the same. He could talk to anyone, and he did. All ages, all walks of life, men and women, young and old – people were drawn to him.

I saw Michael as being very patient and kind with all people – the sweet old lady, the middle-aged woman behind the counter at the post office, the mechanic, the delivery person, the parents of his children's friends, and anyone else he came across in his travels. Michael was strict with his boundaries, and he had such a creative way of helping people to become aware of their inappropriate behaviour, if that was required. He would do this in such a way that people suddenly became incredibly self-aware, seeing themselves too clearly to defend their behaviour, sheepishly or surprisingly accepting the reflection which was on offer.

Michael is a man of harmony – he will always choose the peaceful road if it will result in more love. He would never intentionally cause harm, and, in fact, he intentionally attempts to never cause harm. He seeks to uplift and to share a little experience of his inner reality, without ever overstepping, without ever a trace of superiority, and without ever proclaiming anything from a soap box. Michael impacts people through his living, through his example, and through the simplicity of his day-to-day activities. Rather than being forced or demanded, Michael simply allows love to flow forth from him, filling the space around him, and being freely and unconditionally shared.

Michael meets and accepts all people exactly where they are at, and he speaks with ease and interest about their subject or area of expertise. I still aspire to that level of communication. He really just loves people, and his loving them raises them up. To love is effortless for Michael – it is his favourite thing to do, as natural and as simple as taking his next breath.

I remember the first time I got up on stage in front of a crowd to run a healing journey process. It was at an event with many people present. Michael introduced me and when I got to him, I wanted him to stay with me. I previously thought that I would not want him to see how nervous I was or how not yet competent I felt, being in front of him and all those people. Facilitation came so naturally to him, and at first, I felt like I wanted to practice and get good at it before he witnessed me in action. But once I was up on that stage, I quickly changed my mind.

Michael was so supportive, and it felt like he was helping to prepare me for the upcoming work I would be doing with people. He felt so brotherly, like how an older brother supporting his younger sister would feel. I felt really held and championed in this level of support. I felt like I could be here and take on this challenge, whilst also feeling like I had no idea and like I was completely out of my depth. My experience was like having the kindest, most caring, encouraging and supportive friend by my side.

I felt his protection as well, and I felt safe to settle and be there, and I didn't care that he could really see me. I was exposed to him, and this was the safest place to be. This was the best place for me to be courageous and to begin. Not feeling competent or ready didn't really factor into it; I was here, and the moment was now. Michael hovered for a time while I settled myself and "got out of the way", opening to the channel.

Michael then slipped to the back of the room and, while I was in the process with the people, I could also feel and had a clear example of him holding space – of him holding the protection field and the healing/clearing energies with me and the people. Being able to energetically facilitate with Michael and feeling, firsthand, how he works with various energies, was incredibly insightful. His energetic capacity is enormous and diverse, and he is very deliberate and considerate in how he works with energy.

Michael possesses a fearlessness, a steadfastness and a calm assurance which is completely void of arrogance or self-importance. He feels genuinely grateful and humbled to be working with energy and with people, unafraid and fiercely protective, whilst also extending deep nurturance and genuine interest.

I have learned a lot, from Michael, about interdimensional communications and channellings.

These experiences with Michael were a huge and important source of learning and growth for me. I was often "put on the spot" or "thrown in the deep end". But through this, I got to face some of my most mortifying challenges and deepest fears. I was never forced into anything, but when the timing of the opportunity was ripe, it was magic, really, and I always wanted to explore what I was capable of.

in a benevolent universe (and a fourth-ray system), I am very grateful for these experiences which, on my own, I would not have been able to embrace due to my passivity, my sensitivity and my receptivity imbalances. Before meeting Michael, I was always waiting to be ready, never feeling competent enough, and not feeling good enough in general. Without guidance, I just didn't have the active drive or the courage or the ability in my make-up and my expression (being still weighted with trauma, wounding and introversion) to go forth and have these experiences.

On my own, I always felt like I didn't have it in me to initiate the action which was necessary to face and embrace such challenges. Nor did I feel like I had the strength to face my fears and really step up and into myself. So, the push (or shall I say the active encouragement) was always timely and necessary. Without Michael's encouragement, I never would have pushed the bounds of what I believed to be possible. I never would have challenged myself and overcome what I have. And for that, I am deeply grateful.

Prior to meeting Michael and beginning the work of psychological clearing and healing, I was a passenger in my life. I was overly sensitive and introverted, crippled by my severe shyness. I remain so grateful, filled with deep respect and appreciation, to have received the guidance of a teacher such as Michael, and to have had such opportunities for learning and growth. I have had opportunity after opportunity and experience after experience to heal and grow and become more of what and who I really am, so that I may longer and better serve. What a gift.

And, some 26 years after that fateful first meeting with Michael, we're still just getting started – the journey continues as it began.

STORY TWO

~ ~ ~

The day I reconnected with Michael in February 2001, through a wondrous series of synchronicities, there was immediate recognition. We talked and I felt that I had come home. Michael asked about my health, what I had been doing with my life, and we shared intuitive insights while discovering a common bond of the love of Spirit and of service, very much like old friends. Michael asked if I would be interested in joining his spiritual mentoring program, which made my heart sing, and so began many changes that continue rippling out to this day, for life would never be the same again.

We discussed the upcoming Wesak Festival at Mount Shasta in northern California that was mentioned on his website, and everything came together when I shared that I strongly felt to participate, at which point Michael kindly offered accommodation in a house he had already booked.

Life quickened and three months later my husband and I found ourselves sharing a house with Michael, his family and other students who had arrived to participate in the annual Wesak Festival. The festival is also known, to many, as the Buddha's birthday and it is a time of potential spiritual initiation, when humanity is offered the opportunity to progress on the spiritual path depending on choices made over the past year.

It was a wonderful experience being with hundreds of spiritual aspirants from all over the world, and a great opportunity to learn and to begin to expand into levels of awareness that had been just out of reach up until then. Each day there were new speakers and energy activations, gifted new age musicians and stalls selling beautiful crystals and books written about ascension, though it was the inner experiences that had a profound impact on my heart and reality.

The day following the event, our group was invited to attend a meeting with the leadership team of the organization that had facilitated the Wesak Festival. This became an opportunity to observe the presenters and musicians in a more relaxed environment compared to when presenting on stage, and there were a few surprises. When reviewing the day, I was shown that my unfounded expectations, when mixed in with my tendency to put spiritual teachers up on a pedestal (which isn't kind to either of us, as no one is perfect), limits the potential wisdom that can be shared between awakening and evolving souls.

After many lives of devotion to something or someone whom I believed superior, whether it be academically, spiritually or both, this topic has been an ongoing challenge for me. Now twenty years down the track, I can see how Michael allowed the devotion for a time, while also gradually disclosing its limitations. When coming from a distorted motivation, devotion can become disempowering as we give our power over to another. Ultimately, as we begin walking the spiritual path, our devotion reorients to the sacred spark – to the God Within.

The following day my husband and I flew across the US to Florida for a holiday, though it became a very different experience from what had been anticipated, for the reality of leaving a very spiritually pure energy space in the mountains to step into the hype of Disney World could not have been more extreme. Everything felt abrasive, as though my skin had been removed, and I just wanted to return to the stillness of the mountains and forest. Many deep breaths, along with listening to the energy clearing CD I had bought, helped a lot. I certainly came home challenged and changed, for some of the old veils had dropped to assist me in seeing just where I was at.

In other words, how much love compared to fear was I holding? And at that time the levels of fear were rising strongly, as can happen when much change and transformation is occurring.

Prior to working with Michael, I had spent three seven-year cycles studying and facilitating with four other spiritual groups and I 'thought' that I had a pretty good grip on spiritual topics. Well, this was a bubble which was due to burst, for spiritual growth is made through the heart rather than the mind, which is a whole new reality for sure. This came as somewhat of a reality check, for in coming to no longer allow what I 'know' to define me, I was able to experience the alchemical refinement which spurs spiritual evolution – a process which can only occur through the heart, through love rather than through mental activity.

Upon arriving home, Michael emailed to say that he knew I had been through a challenge and to invite me over for lunch, where we spoke about how important it was to be more grounded in my life now. We spoke about plans for the future, about establishing a weekly class, and about how to be more present so as to not be so affected by other people's energy and moods, and by the phenomena in my life. This was such a gift, for at the time I was often knocked off centre by taking on other people's energy and emotions, which left me wondering why I was all over the place for what seemed to be no apparent reason.

This deeply connected into a warped belief that everyone else was okay, and that I was dysfunctional – a belief that many of us who are sensitive have adopted as a coping strategy when life suddenly hits us in the face while we're still young.

Due to our young age, we may not yet have the capacity to process our response to a world which can oftentimes feel brutal, and so we take the line of least resistance and choose fear over love. It feels easier to blame ourselves than to find a way to remain in integrity, compassion and love as we remove our rose-coloured glasses and observe the world as it truly is, acknowledging and accepting people for how they really are, dysfunction and all. Dependent as we are upon the people around us, we want to believe that they are good and loving and that we can follow their lead. And so, we take them at their word, convincing ourselves that they know best, learning how to keep them pleased with us, and navigating by external cues rather than the knowing of our own hearts.

The journey of review and the process of retracing our steps to regain and nurture self-worth, remembering how to trust and to navigate by the knowing of the heart, is unique to each of us. Though not necessarily easy, I came to learn that it certainly can be done. With the Masters showing us the way through the maze, guiding us to the light within the heart once more, we can return to ourselves.

This, to me, means the restoration of hope, which is no small thing, and within my heart I hold eternal gratitude to the teachers who have paved the way for each of us.

Michael had not long moved to Melbourne from New South Wales and was looking for a venue to start weekly classes, so I offered him the teaching room in my home which was in the forest on the side of Mount Dandenong, where I had been facilitating classes.

And so began a whole new journey of self-discovery that continues to this day.

I really had no idea what was before me in terms of how the ascension-descension process works – I just wanted to rediscover the magic that had felt missing for so long, and to then be able to make a difference in the world with greater clarity, joy and love.

After years of struggling with my marital relationship, and after months of deep inner reflection, I realised that I had been avoiding the inevitable and I made the hard choice of separation. I wish to make it clear, here, that this decision was mine alone. I have only ever received unconditional support from Michael, and far from interfering in the lives of his students, he attempts only to encourage us to seek out the potential lessons, growth and transformation in whatever situations we find ourselves. Michael advocates for seeking harmony and achieving mastery in all things.

Life, as I had known it, changed yet again.

This was a very challenging time. One of endings and new beginnings, of learning how to keep my head above water while living a very different life with different interactions and judgments from family and friends. My heart knew that it was time to separate, for my own wellbeing, though that was not understood by many who had been close to me both socially and spiritually. In review, it took time to reconcile the grief of endings and the inspiration and passion to commit fully to the spiritual path and self-mastery, for they seemed somewhat at odds with each other. Many of us have this split between the priorities of the Spiritual and the desire for a successful human life wavering within us, though with guidance and commitment this can be healed to allow a natural flow of life through all our experiences.

In order to become truly integrated, the human life must become spiritualised. To answer the call of Spirit should, indeed, ripple out and transform the human life, but one should not detract from the other. The human life should become an avenue for spiritual exploration and evolution – an opportunity to ground and express love, to live as an initiate on planet earth where the initiate is most needed – and the process of becoming spiritually motivated should uplift and enrich the human life. To become an initiate is to walk the talk of self-mastery. It is to embody and to reflect the spiritual through all aspects of human life. It is to live an ordinary life in an extraordinary way.

We moved the class to a new venue nearby, and Michael and his wife kindly offered accommodation while I found a sweet cottage by the sea as my new home. This was the first time I had lived alone in 54 years and so much was changing now on so many levels. It became clear that it was well time to let go and to receive loving kindness with much gratitude. Here began a very new experience of unconditional love from others, and eventually from and for myself. It can be a bit of a bumpy road when old beliefs around being unlovable raise their heads to push away love, especially when the love is given freely with no expectation of return, but with firm and loving guidance and persistence, these feelings of being unlovable can become healed.

Choosing to study with an initiate brings a plethora of experiences as we open to higher inspiration and new learning. There is yet another aspect which is equally profound, and that is the opportunity to work with the inner plane beings and energies that most of us have heard of, though not experienced on the ground. These beings are not as far away as we may think, and the experience of being held in unconditionally loving energies while undergoing the ascension alchemical process is really an incredible blessing.

This is the magic that I had felt to be missing for most of this life before finding a teacher who could reconnect me with an almost forgotten part of myself once again. For this, I am ever grateful and truly inspired along the way.

There are many opportunities to choose joy.

Each week, five of us climbed into the car and drove the hour to class and what a wondrous opportunity this was to let go of old concepts of who and what an initiate was and is.

Sometimes Michael generously shared some of his own experiences from his early years, of his teachers, of past lives that were relevant, of insights into the events of the world, his preparation for the future, and far more. Other times, there was silence and the opportunity to just be together in the beautiful energy of stillness.

Following class, much to my horror at the time (after years of being involved in natural medicine), we would drive to a nearby McDonald's for a late dinner and here I discovered, yet again, to never try to put anyone in a box – especially one who is a few steps ahead, for nothing is as it seems. This is one of Michael's gifts – to live an ordinary life in an extraordinary way as he shows us how to do the same, encouraging us to burst out of our old self-limiting beliefs of who and what we think we are, and of what we can and can't do and be.

It took me a while, but once I had moved beyond my own initial judgments, I recognised the innocence, the beauty, and the intention in those late-night visits to McDonald's. Michael's son, who had recently turned 16, had become interested in his spiritual development and had begun attending Michael's weekly classes. His son loved spending time with his dad, and, like every 16-year-old teenager, he loved dining out. And so, it turned out, a McDonald's dinner was something both exceedingly normal and very simple that Michael could do for and with his son. Sometimes, the most meaningful and significant gestures are the simplest ones.

This was a way that Michael could connect with his son, joyfully supporting and celebrating his spiritual growth and development, whilst simultaneously encouraging intimacy, love and connection amongst his students. Michael's great love even extended to include the McDonald's staff, and they all inevitably smiled and relaxed as he invited them to partake of the magic of those encounters.

Those meals came to be some of the most joy-filled and exuberant displays of love that I had ever born witness to.

Through this, I learned the significance of creating outcomes of love. Far from being prudish, dogmatic, judgmental and stuck up (traits I had grown accustomed to in various spiritual communities), Michael was grounded, down-to-earth, and enabling love in even the most simple of ways.

Michael offers the gift of 'no limits!'. How can anything or anyone change and ultimately evolve, when held in a small mental box? This includes each one of us, for as I have learned over the years, we are all unique in our journey, experience, gifts and ultimate purpose, rather like different colours in a kaleidoscope that creates a beautiful and intricate pattern as the light – Spirit – shines through it.

The ascension process is somewhat different to what I had studied previously, though it became apparent that the years spent with other teachers had been wondrous preparation for where I was now, and I am ever grateful for the guidance of the Universe. Michael facilitates an ascending-descension process, which emphasises the necessity of transforming the human vehicle through psychological insight and clarity, through a raising and refinement of vibration, through the process of actualisation (rather than mere realisation), as well as through complete and thorough embodiment, in order to become safe host for Spirit. Rather than ascending out, exiting the wheel of death and rebirth and escaping to higher planes of existence, Michael's approach is grounded and service-oriented – ready the vehicle, and allow Spirit to ground here, expressing through you, unafraid and embracing all parts of the human experience. Rather than being a process of getting "out", it is a process of coming all the way "in".

In saying that, one of the first realizations I had was that it was time to let go of all that I 'thought' I knew, and to make way for new learning. The first step was humbling, as is often the way, when I was shown that I was not at all grounded.

'Of course I am grounded; I have physically helped build two houses, I have birthed and brought up two children, and I have dealt with life's many challenges!', I defended.

Well, the point was that at that time in my life, I, as the soul, spent most of my time behind my body wondering what "I" will do next, and it was well time to be in the driver's seat once again. I will admit that giving up chanting and changing my meditation technique rankled somewhat, for it was a wonderful escape to bliss out in other realities. What is really needed, however, is to bring the love here now, grounded and expressed by walking the talk as it were.

Michael offered a great gift in helping me come to this understanding through what he shares and how he lives, consciously choosing the highest possible outcome always, regardless of the phenomena happening around him. Love knows the way through!

I remembered being told by a previous teacher that, 'I cannot give you anything new when you come with both hands already full!'.

This was the beginning of the "unbecoming" that the Masters speak of in the ancient texts, when all that is known is surrendered to All That Is.

Over the years Michael has patiently reminded us that genuine respect, gratitude and humility are doorways to greater realities within and without of us, and that each of us is more capable than we are aware. I remember reading that the qualities one perceives in another are already held within, otherwise we could not recognize them. Once perceived, it becomes our responsibility to actualise and to bring those qualities to the fore. A juicy thought to ponder on, perhaps.

I have learned, through experience in other spiritual groups, that there can be a tendency for the group leaders and teachers to live two separate lives, in a way – one when on stage, channelling the higher energies while facilitating for students, and another when off the stage and socialising.

When one is offering a new way of higher truth and love, there is a responsibility to walk the talk. Leaders and teachers should maintain high ethics and morals as an inspiration for the who are a few steps behind, living as an example of integrity, and embodying those on-stage channellings.

With Michael, there is no pretence – you get what you see. He makes a point of avoiding hypocrisy by holding himself to high standards. As his students, we know and witness that he would never ask a thing of us which he, himself, is not embodying. He is, on the stage, as he is in his day-to-day life. Bridging all gaps and transcending those splits which I had witnessed in other spiritual groups, Michael is authentic in his grounded and genuinely love-motivated approach to all areas of his life. His fearlessness, his integrity, his robustness and his authenticity are both refreshing and inspiring.

In the weekly classes, Michael covered many topics including energy hygiene and the importance of maintaining appropriate boundaries from a place of self-love. It was again humbling to discover that a lot of the mood swings, anger, sadness, frustration, headaches etc, which were a common experience, often weren't mine at all, and how I could change this tendency to take on other people's energy by being present. It is empowering to reclaim one's energy consciously, rather than hoping the disharmony will go away, or that someone will come along to fix it. This new understanding also brought me the courage to stay true to my heart while maintaining stronger boundaries from self-love, rather than taking a deep dive into other people's realities and getting sideswept by my own layers of guilt at the time.

There was a belief in the back of my mind that once one had committed to the Spiritual Path, then everything suddenly became a wondrous journey of self-discovery, and all became right with the world. However, this is somewhat of a fairytale, for to walk the Spiritual Path, one must undertake the inner journey of evolution through transformation and alchemy and, as I discovered, this journey is totally unique for each of us and can, at times, be extremely challenging (depending on the stability of our self-worth).

Over time, Michael shared tools and processes that were the preparation to be able to facilitate the Cosmosis® process – personal spiritual alchemy – for oneself from the very beginning. By using this process, we develop the ability to hold steady when challenged or in pain in any way, and to expand our capacity to love beyond the consuming fears that we carry within. This is an empowering but confronting process which can be challenging for the ego, and, for this reason, it is not for the feint hearted. Though love and light always direct and motivate this process, its success requires the ferocity of the love and light of a Spiritual Warrior – fearless, unwavering, and powerful.

I love the saying, "The degree of challenge and fear is indicative of the potential for love!". It's essential to remember that it's all just energy, and that we each have more courage than we know!

Cosmosis® has been an incredible gift of grace, for it offers healing on a very deep level of emotional, mental and spiritual wounding, from this and other lives. This is what I had been seeking all my life, in fact – it is the return to the magic of wholeness!

Each week I witnessed the capacity for unconditional love that Michael holds for his students and for all life. Having been somewhat wary for a while, due to previous experience in other spiritual organizations, the experience I was having with Michael brought hope to my heart that there are teachers out there who practice what they preach. This is the hallmark of a Spiritual initiate – that they uplift their students by being a grounded example of one who walks the talk no matter what is going on within or around them. You see, in this way they become way showers for others, and they demonstrate that there is always the potential of a better way – a way of higher love – and that we are all capable of coming fully to the embodiment of this reality.

One of my biggest learnings in the early days was that Michael does not judge anyone for their mistakes or choices. Being truthful, it took many years for me to accept that this applies to me as well, for judgment had become my first reach when feeling out of my depth. Many times, after making a mistake or missing an opportunity, I felt Damocles' sword hanging over my head, when in truth it was only my old programming of self-judgment which I'd learned in the earlier years of my life from a highly critical parent who was adept at maintaining guilt for days (and even weeks) after a mistake was made. It has taken time to heal the layers of this old belief, for it ran deep.

I remember missing a spiritual test when one weekend, around three months after my separation, I invited my kids and grandkids for lunch for my birthday, forgetting that it was the weekend of a new age fair in the local town and that I had volunteered to support a stall held by Michael's wife to offer spiritual services and promote his classes. All went well on the Saturday. It was quiet, so I checked in with her that it would be okay to stay home the next day to try to make peace with my family after having separated recently from my husband. I was still new to the group and didn't realize that one of the classic tests early on the path is of holding to a commitment to service, regardless of external phenomena.

The following week, Michael was standing outside when I pulled up for class. He took me aside to gently clarify that I had chosen fear and guilt over love, and I waited for the sword to fall. To my surprise, all that was offered by Michael was kindness and encouragement to do better next time. Being used to having my head bitten off in the past, this was a very new experience, I can tell you.

Far from the guilt trips I had come to expect from my previous relationships, Michael simply helped me to see that, whilst harmonising my relationship with my family and spending time sharing love with them was a kind and worthwhile thing to do, I needed to be more aware of my time management and my prior commitments, because although this was a small service project, sometimes larger service projects will require energy, attention and focus, and it is through these smaller service projects that we build, develop, and demonstrate our prior commitment to service. To be able and willing to follow through is a fine and necessary spiritual requirement.

Time and again, I have witnessed unconditional reflections, support and encouragement from Michael, with never a trace of judgment, malice, or manipulation. Michael uses every situation as an opportunity to teach, support and encourage growth in his students.

As time progressed, the inspiration landed to offer a two-day Spiritual Ascension Festival, similar to the Wesak Festival in California. The public were invited to participate in talks on ascension, to experience spiritual energy activations, to hear great music, and to explore beautiful stalls offering crystals and handmade arts and crafts. As invited, the group pulled together international musicians and speakers. It was a wonderful weekend where we all played our part selling tickets, housing performers, giving talks, and meeting many people who were open to experiencing a new way of life. The event brought many challenges, copious learning and much joy as I began to feel the warmth of belonging to a group of like-minded souls who were open to new learning, while holding the vision of giving back to this beautiful planet.

I have learned that of course there will be challenges, for that is life happening, and that it is up to each of us to choose how we respond to life's challenges. As we rise to the challenge, we rise on the path of Spiritual Initiation to embody higher levels of truth, which opens us up to the potential embodiment of higher love. This takes time, for we are each a unique work in progress. One of my biggest learnings has been to summon my will, to be courageous enough to stay through the times when I am really challenged, to choose to do it differently, and to not collapse into the comfort zone of old behaviour patterns which I have the opportunity to now move beyond. It's pretty wild sometimes, the knots we have tied ourselves up in.

One of the things I am most grateful for is Michael's ability to translate complex esoteric teachings into an evening's class that is comprehensible to everyone. This is a great gift given and received, to be able to take new understanding into our hearts anew, and our gift back is to then share that gift from the heart, as new hope for many.

As the years passed, Michael felt to take the teachings to Perth to begin a new centre there, and another student and I were offered the opportunity to take over the lease of his home from which to facilitate ongoing meditation classes, workshops and healing sessions. It was a wonderful opportunity and a joyful learning curve of coordinating speakers, classes, sessions and events.

A couple of years later I was offered the opportunity to also move to Perth to work at a women's gym, and I jumped at it for it was another new beginning in my life. Driving alone across the Nullarbor Plain brought a heart opening sense of freedom and, in retrospect, I wish I had taken longer to embrace the journey more deeply, though at the time I was on a mission and made it across in four days.

We live on a wondrous and deeply spiritual land of ancient peoples and traditions, with a sky so enormous that it seems to go on forever, bringing a feeling of expanded oneness and filling the spaces of seeming nothingness, both within and without.

I didn't feel alone for one minute, for I could feel the energies we are so blessed to work with at the Cosmosis® Mentoring Centre, travelling with me always – guiding, offering insight and unconditional love – and this sense has never left me, even after twenty-three years. I am never alone. I am always loved and supported along the journey.

Michael's mentoring has birthed transformation within as I engage with the alchemical processes he selflessly shares. Learning to release the judgment that maintains separation from love is a big one. Psychological clarity is essential, and the journey from the racing egoic mind and back to the stillness held within the heart calls forth courage and commitment to the highest love and truth, and is so very worth it's attainment.

Each is a step into wholeness and evolution from which to embrace a long-standing passion to give back to this beautiful sphere called earth, as she returns once more to sacred status through the power of love. This is what truly makes my heart sing on so many levels and beyond.

The journey continues with challenges woven in, with deep gratitude, wonder and joy!

Never alone, always one within the many.

STORY THREE

~ ~ ~

"Stop imagining and experience the real."
- Michael King

Beyond the Fairytale

   I suspect that the best, most unexpected thing that's happened so far in this life is finding a clear mirror that knows me better than I know myself, and getting busy knowing myself in the reflection.
   I found this mirror in Michael, the first time, without even knowing it. I was in Northern California, searching for "home", 6 years before I finally found it. It was 2001 and I had packed up and said goodbye -again- to my hometown friends and my family in Rhode Island. I could not ignore the call that made every other option pale into nonsense. I was weaving my way along, following a whisper in my heart. Sometimes it was clear, and sometimes it was completely constructed from my delusions, but the universe, being benevolent, somehow wove together each thread of those murmurings, moving me toward the amazing life that I live today.
   A group from Australia was attending the Wesak event in Mount Shasta. I had just heard of this celebration and that

there would be a lot of people worth meeting there. In one particular case, that was the understatement of a lifetime.

I had no idea why, but I knew I was to attend. I had one contact, a friend of a friend, who I could stay with. It all flowed into place, as though it was "meant to be". The festival was held in a big auditorium in the little town at the foot of the mountain. It felt like a little mecca for the New Age movement.

Throughout the weekend, I kept bumping into one woman and we'd lock eyes. It was one of the only things I remember from the whole time I was there. We would heart link, communing energetically. Each time we crossed paths, I was somehow stopped in my tracks – a mutual recognition. Over the three days, I do not think we exchanged a single word until the last day when we had a long-lost-friend kind of hug and she pushed me back, held me at arm's length, and said, 'We will see each other again.' I said, 'Yes, I don't know how, but I know we will.' I simply KNEW her beyond the moment. I knew her as a soul, an old friend, a heart so familiar, a member of my spiritual family. I couldn't imagine living my life without seeing her and her people. That made no sense to me, because they lived on the opposite side of the planet, so I let that go, choosing to align myself to the highest love for all concerned, and I am so glad that I did.

That Wesak full moon, in the auditorium, I was told there was a very interesting guy, a highly respected and adept initiate from Australia, Michael King, running a meditation, and that I should not miss that session. I heard Michael's voice, and it was like I was waking from a dream. He was inviting people to settle in. Were there a thousand people in the room that day? It seemed like a lot! When I closed my eyes, though, I was overcome by a sense that there were thousands more, a massive crowd flooding in, on the inner planes.

The lights were dim, and a violet hue filled the room. I was at the back. I felt like I was witnessing something truly big, shifting my whole world; something that I could not fathom. It was the strangest thing at the time. I looked around to see if others were noticing this. Everyone seemed unaffected, relaxed, most with their eyes closed. I don't know what happened when I heard him begin the process. I felt like I was magnetically drawn into my seat, sucked into place, anchored down and snapped to attention. I felt like a cold, crisp, clarity was washed through me. It commanded my respect, and I was very grateful to give it. My inner eyes widened like I was remembering, but I had no idea what.

It was a steely, sharp contrast to what I had experienced for as long as I could remember, and different to all the other presenters I had witnessed at this event. I was used to feeling floaty and all "love and light"-y. A midwife friend used to say I was "going transparent", that she could practically see through me, that I needed to eat meat and get my feet on the ground because I was floating away. Wise words in hindsight. This clarity-feeling was not familiar, but it was very welcome.

Michael's voice was potent, powerful, real, different. There was this feeling of being totally accepted and seen for who I was, rather than for who I was wanting to be. I was being seen through all my bullshit, but I was not being judged. Everything I had hidden from myself and from others was washed with this clear light, and it was okay.

It all happened so fast. Talk about stopped in my tracks. It felt like my energy was aligning. I was clicking into place, grounding into my physical body and into the Earth more than I ever had. I was a bit confused, and I almost laughed out loud because I heard a voice so loudly and clearly that it startled me. 'Hello.' I was having a clear conversation inside, with a very loving being. Maybe it was Michael. It was certainly associated with him.

Michael's voice carried over the PA, soaking the room, steady and deliberate. Every word was landing like a crystalline note, piercing my hazy mind. The accent, the tone, the deep and very simple but extraordinary content of the discourse were so familiar, and yet so new that I needed to focus on this voice. I could not see the stage. It was as though he was speaking from within my heart. It was a feeling process, at least for me. There were invocations and a calling in of higher energies and I recognised that this, what this voice was saying, was everything that I was looking for. I don't remember any of the words, except for a few names, but I do remember the feeling. It was like true north.

The process was long. I remember feeling like I was walking with him, skipping through and beyond time in the meditation. He was talking straight to me and yet everyone else on the inner and in the room could perhaps feel that way, too. I was wondering how I would ever be able to manifest what this voice, this being, was opening the door on as an option to choose. I absolutely wanted to live in the world that this guy was aiming for and calmly spelling out as though it was already done. There was no question that this person had blueprints that could work; he had mapped out very clear solutions that did not miss steps.

I was so full of energy – I understood everything he said but could not remember anything he said. It felt like he was speaking a language that a part of me completely understood, but one which the part of me that was in the chair was struggling to make out. I just knew that this was way more sense than my heart had ever heard before, and I had been searching already for a long time. I put my hand up on the inner, proclaiming a big and heart-resounding 'YES'. I wanted to be part of this. Yes, I wanted to hear more of what that voice had to say.

Then it was over. It took me a while to stand. I wanted to stay there. It felt warm; soul-warming, lung-filling, like a blast of air; like when you dive deep and a bit too long underwater, then burst through the surface and gulp in the sky. I didn't realise I had been under for so long. Meeting Michael, that first time, was a culmination of instant recognition and instant 'yes please, more of this.' I don't know if upstairs or Michael heard me, or if I heard them. All I know is, I heard the call and by some miracle they heard my answer.

It is extraordinary to look back over that period of my life with the kind of hindsight that comes with studying under Michael King and the Cosmosis® Mentoring Centre for the last two decades. So many insights later, I can breathe and reflect on the tapestry of learning that arises through this path of transformation.

Since meeting Michael, every part of my perception of the world and of myself has become clearer, and more aligned to common sense and the laws of physics. Reviewing the magnitude of a rather constant influx of pivotal moments makes me want to burst out laughing and crying with gratitude. I see now how every word, every speck of interaction with Michael, was designed to make me stronger, wiser and fitter for awakening to my potential. By following his example of so clearly seeing the world as it is, I have gathered more and more courage to welcome the truth. This astoundingly growth-enriched chapter of my life emerged from such a generous offering from this truly illumined soul.

After that original Wesak experience, a series of events unfolded as the fervour of my pursuit to find a soul partner (the next step in my "dream life" plan) leapt into high gear. I embarked on quite an exquisitely painful journey, discovering what happens when one follows the "enthusiasm of the gonads" but dresses it up as spirituality, metaphysics and higher calling. My ego was in full flight, with the best of New Age intentions, and I had no understanding of boundaries or psychological clarity.

Therein lay the recipe for some big and soul-changing lessons that I was calling in and manifesting for myself.

It has taken me the best part of twenty years to accept and to be okay with where I was at then, deep in a fantasy life. I learned from some of Michael's discourses about a psychological and spiritual pathology called a high-low split – a schism which separates the higher and the lower, holding the inner and the outer apart from each other so that two separate realities are experienced instead of a single, synthesised and integrated one. There was a rather gaping high-low split that I needed to bridge and heal to even begin to peer beyond my "happily ever after" scripts, even though I was parading around and pretending that I was an empowered, free, spiritual woman.

I was following Spirit with a broken barometer that told me love equals sex and that I needed a partner to be able to follow the calling in my heart. The "high" in that split can be described as having a "rose coloured glasses" view of the world. This view showed only what I wanted to see, the potential of what I knew I could be, and what I imagined others could be if they got the "right kind of love". This attitude was encouraged in the circles that I found myself drawn to as I searched for "something more" – I always felt that I needed *more* to fill the bottomless pit of low self-esteem.

The "low" end of the split had that protective mechanism of spiritual glamour, false humility and sweet frosting to cover up my feelings of worthlessness, my impure motives, and my deep self-loathing as I dragged the past along. All of this self-inflicted drama, especially the giving my love and my body away, was, sadly, extremely destructive to me as a soul and as a woman. As it turns out, it was delusional rather than virtuous to believe that everyone was good at heart and just needed more love. I wasn't simple – I was not so innocent – I was just rejecting the truth to avoid the pain of facing myself and reality.

Choosing to avoid and deny reality took its toll; I knocked myself around and I left myself open as a target to be knocked around. I believed my own bullshit, so it was easy to go into agreement with bullshit from others as well. I was loath to accept the truth of what was right there in plain view in front of me – the evidence of the experience I'd had in my own body, mind and spirit, when I was sitting in that auditorium with Michael.

Rather than face it at that juncture, I chose to fortify my wish life. I rejected my true self and the guidance that was pointing me always toward my ability to take responsibility for my life, my karma, and my prior commitments. Unconsciously, I was still entangled in the saviourship model of spirituality. I was waiting for a Messiah. My New Age, arrogant, inflated ego would settle for nothing less, and I was not even patient enough to wait.

Rather than following my heart's knowing, I answered my ego's urges. Soon after my experience at Mount Shasta, I found myself a stand-in saviour – a spiritual and romantic partner who matched my unclarity and dysfunction. I found a mirror of trauma and of drama, of self-loathing and personal myths, and I ran straight at that mirror, colliding with it headfirst, partnering up in weakness and believing that it would bring me the answers that I had been seeking. Then, I got pregnant and played out a hefty circuitous journey that exposed quite the cache of wisdom, acquired through conflict, as I made my way through the labyrinth of my own beliefs, making pathways to self-mastery.

In my stupor, I completely forgot about that Wesak encounter with "true north" as I tripped over my avoidance and denial, until eventually landing in a heap at the doorway to my destiny. I was so ungrounded at that time of my life. I had become a quintessential new age hippie-girl – a shaman-flavoured spiritual midwife, gypsy-ing around the world listening to the call of babies who wanted me at their births. Even as I acted out as a wounded ego, the call to get myself into place, to serve, to step onto the path, was getting stronger.

Everything else just felt pointless and miserable. I was fighting to wake up from the self-imposed limitation of my embarrassing addiction to secretly pursuing "true love." I know this has been a pitfall of mine for many lifetimes. I was born looking for my "true love", and only meeting Michael was able to break that curse. But it took years of looking in all the wrong places to find him again.

I felt the calling for years, but I was obsessed with finding my soul mate and building my wish life, believing that, once I had those things secured, my partner and I could go and find where our home was. I also had a primal soul narrative that I would be okay and that I would be able to switch on once I found my knight in shining armour. I simultaneously judged this as weak and pathetic, but I felt like I needed to follow this call, wherever it took me.

Like so many budding lightworkers, while my idea of commitment to service was full of great intentions, my actions and my lack of discipline set me on a long, harmful journey, replete with the rich and painful learnings that arise from stubborn New Age entitlement. When the call came early in my life, my heart was so intoxicated by the glamour and illusion and maya of the human desires, and I became so attached to dabbling in sex as a way to achieve enlightenment, that I did not recognise many of the signposts, nudges to maintain hope, and opportunities to demonstrate self-mastery along the way.

By the time I showed up in Mount Shasta, I thought that I was there to find the life partner who would lead me to the "Path". So convinced was I that, when the path presented, despite being able to recognise it and despite feeling as though I had found my teacher, I could not imagine a world where it was that simple. I only had eyes for the glamour of the fairytale. I had answered the call but then only heard what I wanted to hear, and I placed conditions on answering the call – 'Only once I have found my true love! Only once the fairytale is complete!'

Fortunately, though, "the call" rising from within me and the benevolence that had answered both knew my heart. Some part of me had never given up, had never forgotten why I was here. I truly wanted to find the path, clear my dysfunctions, and make myself fit for service in this life. I knew I had to say no to a happily ever after, that I had to surrender the American dream and the white picket fence, but I kept behaving like that was all I wanted.

How did the years pass so quickly? I wasted so much time living my "I'll have my cake and eat it too" life. I was living life on ego's terms rather than life on life's terms, as Michael suggests.

This was the question ringing through me some years later, around Wesak time in May of 2004. I found myself face down on the very vibrant 70's carpet on the floor of my loungeroom, having a mini bardo experience. I had just gotten my 4-month-old baby to fall asleep after a long time of trying everything I could think of. As a professional midwife and experienced bodyworker, having this colicky, very unsettled baby felt quite desperately challenging to my self-concept. When everything I had in my toolbelt failed to calm the baby, I was confused, shocked, and dismayed.

Doubt crept in so ferociously. I felt my perceived reality falling away. The very most important thing to me – loving and nurturing life, being an agent of love and light, parenting the new – all seemed far-fetched and out of touch now. I felt powerless and on the brink of despair, even with all my life experience which included thousands of hours of labours, over four hundred births (which were mostly homebirths), many hundreds of hours of holding bodies of all kinds through massage, bodywork, healing, transformation, birthing and dying... and here I was.

 The baby didn't care a hoot about my credentials. He was just getting it all out. That newborn baby cry has special power. Having half my DNA, his cries tugged on my physiology, my psyche, my soul. I found myself in a total stress response spiral. I was shrouded in a drama of my own making, and I was completely devastated. I was entering dangerous levels of sleep deprivation and depression. I had so firmly believed my inner myth and fairytale. I had lived a wish life, hoping my dreams would all come true, and here I was, in my very high flying, brightly joyful and glowing "spiritual" life, crashed in a heap from a great height.

 I was experiencing a collapse of the high-low split. I could feel the love and joy to have this little baby in my life AND I could feel the loss of opportunity. I could feel the devastation of irresponsible and lose-lose choices which were, in hindsight, very foolish. Life was a complete mist. I was sinking. I knew I came to this world with a purpose, a reason to not just go down the mainstream path. I had a bachelor's degree, with a major in education and a secondary in French teaching. I had degrees and professional certification in massage, and I was a certified professional midwife in the US. I had travelled the world. I had experienced trauma and moved through it, or so I thought. I had studied metaphysics and worked on myself since I was very young. I wanted to serve, and here I was, pathetic. I was so over myself.

 Face down, in front of the little woodstove, in the glow of the orange flames on that carpet, I had a stern talk with God. I am grateful I can laugh now as I feel a surge of compassion and love for that woman, 20 years ago. There I was, having put the baby to sleep at long last, and having a borderline PTSD panic attack, knowing that like the many nights before, I was in for a long one. That night, I knew I was at an unhealthy angle in every way. I was clinging to a ledge that I was already staring over, threatening to tumble to a point of no return. As a soul, in this lifetime, I knew that whatever I chose next would change everything. I felt a clanging truth, that my choices that led to this situation were quite off kilter. I am grateful for all those on the inner and in my life that reached out to steady me and who were there when I reached out that night.

The fire smoke was soothing. The quiet erupted in a slow wave, when I let myself trust what I knew I was seeing, and as I caught myself from falling over that edge. I made a decision to fight. I pounded my fists on the floor and yelled (not loud enough to wake that baby!), at the Universe. I regaled. I writhed. I made a big scene for upstairs. I declared that I knew the truth, that God, that the Universe, that Life and Love were completely benevolent and that I *am* creating my own reality. I hollered that I chose all this! Emphasizing with a little kick. I sat up. I got on my knees in front of that fire. I asked for help. In fact, I demanded help – it was a bit crazy, but I knew that it would take everything I had to get the attention of my upstairs, as I had been such a massively selfish drama queen for the last few years.

I insisted that I changed my mind. 'I choose to get back on track.' I called for help. I had a stab at being as humble as I could. 'I sacrifice my ego completely, take me, I choose to be here as I was called to be, in service to the earth, to Earthbirth, to help to heal sacredness!' I had it out with the Universe. I told her I would give up my bullshit. I would give my life to higher love. I would learn the lessons. I would fight to be a clearer mother, a clearer human.

I asked to be led out of this mess I had made, and I asked for help to have the courage clean up my mess and make myself useful. I was in pain. I was in a severe postnatal depression that I denied because I did not want to hear the cures on offer – drugs, going home to family, giving up my spiritual calling and going to get a job while leaving the baby at home. None of those were an option for me because I knew that all those options led me straight over that cliff. Anything which led me away from the path of the calling was to deny life. I was clear and present with this doomsday feeling, that I would not survive if I took one step further over that ledge.

I sat up. I had that cold clear light feeling. I took a purple pen and paper, and I wrote down all of my declarations and decisions. I made my initials, and I signed it with gratitude to the great love and to the Masters and to the guardian angels and to the Elohim and to all the energies as far and wide and high as I could reach, and to God and the Universe. I sincerely and humbly prostrated myself before the powers of love and beyond. I made a clarion call for help. I sincerely asked for God's will and not my will to be done for the good of all concerned. Then, with a final call and a gratitude prayer, I opened the glass door to the woodstove and threw my letter in to the roaring fire. It was about 10pm in Lake Hawea, New Zealand. I watched that note burn and be delivered to wherever it needed to go.

Another night of breastfeeding, ups and downs, but I woke at 5:30am with adrenaline. I went to the computer and checked my emails. Oddly, there was one from Michael King. After I had moved to New Zealand to have the baby, the baby's father had visited Australia for an event and Michael was made aware of the messy situation. Michael had sent some of his mystery school meditations on CD for me to listen to, and a few months later when the father went travelling, he asked Michael to energetically look after me and the baby. I didn't know this at the time.

Michael had sent me an email at that time, explaining that he was touching base as he was asked to support me as a friend, like a pen pal, and if I needed anything, to reach out.

The email had been very welcomed, I felt a steadying and very kind influence. I was in such a stress state at the time, and I had not completely put together that Michael was that initiate from Mount Shasta. In fact, I had hardly thought of that meditation experience at all. Michael and I had exchanged a couple of emails, I think – just checking in – until that morning, after my rant to the Universe, when another email came through during the night.

The email started with a quick greeting, and then Michael said that the Masters had come to him out of the blue and told him to offer me a scholarship to the Lightworker's program. I sat at the desk staring at the screen in the dawn light. Had I read this correctly? I felt a wave of joy and awe. What? He had heard me. I began to feel that "time standing still" wave wash over me. Everything went quiet. I was anchored into the desk chair. I put it together. This *was* that Michael – the one from Mount Shasta.

He shared some details. It was a one-year program, taking online courses to support psychological clarity, maturity and ethical behaviour in initiates so that they could clear the way to be more solid in their self-esteem foundations and aligned with their service missions. I had not even known he had a school. I had not connected that it was the same Michael, and I was shocked that this high-level initiate would even have the time, or any interest, to email me, let alone offer me his kindness and support. I could feel that same acceptance and non-judgment coming through his words. I remembered in a flash, all that energy of having my hand up and the joy of finding someone whose vision made sense and felt powerfully loving across the board.

Michael's email was simple, clear and concise, and not sympathetic at all. In fact, it was rather empowering. He would require an answer so he could send through a mentoring contract. I felt like the room was filled with light which was spilling out of that email. It was that immediate,

"YES! Hands up!" feeling. I wrote back, thanking him, trying to explain that I had been close to falling over the ledge, and that this was divine timing.

That same day, he sent an attachment with the agreement. In the wording of the agreement, it stated clearly that I would need to let go of my negative ego completely. I swallowed hard. Some of these words were words I had called out last night and declared. I said specifically, 'I will give up my ego! I want to serve, please help me, I want to fulfill my purpose!' I would need to be authentic, or at least working hard toward that. There was a requirement to be living a healthy lifestyle and giving it a go, otherwise it was a waste of time and resources. The ethics were clear and woven through the contract. This was serious. Mostly, I had ticked the boxes: no alcohol whatsoever, no drugs, no smoking, no coffee, no casual sex; basically, no tolerance for behaviours that involve actively poisoning oneself while putting the effort into healing and clearing oneself. It made total sense, and it felt so rare. In all my travels and involvement in spiritual groups, I had not known anyone to hold these kinds of standards and boundaries with their work.

I had goosebumps. In the clear light, my shadow looked way bigger, nastier and disgraceful. Could I really choose this? I felt so worthless in the face of it. This is for real. This is no flippant decision. He is requiring a commitment, to myself, to upstairs, and to him. Signing this meant I was accountable. I couldn't back down without breaking a contract that I had asked for – that I had prayed for. I felt the resistance rise in me. Give UP my ego? I read it again, aloud. Absolutely no tolerance for casual sex – it is listed with the other harmful substances that get in the way of, and are mutually exclusive to, self-mastery. Oh, my, God. I knew I was going to sign it, but I sat with it for a couple of hours to let this sink in.

Another email popped up from Michael. He said I would need to decide soon. He was completely supportive either way, but the energies were holding a door open for me. If I chose to accept the scholarship, I would be working with May and she would get started that next week, walking me through the first course. I knew that this was everything I had been searching for. Just like sitting in that meditation, light years away from this new moment, I knew I wanted to know everything I could about the world view Michael was sharing. I didn't have to tell him about the resistance – he would have felt it. I was feeling so unworthy of this support, but it was so clearly a direction from higher up than my ego, and I had decided that night before to pull myself out of the pits and to give it all I had so that I could keep going and find my way again.

That second email was in the perfect timing to help steady my resolve in the backwash of my fears and the rising tide of doubt. I had gotten into this mess with casual sex and by believing that casual sex was spiritual. I had learned a staunch lesson. I wanted to clean up the mess I had made of this life. Michael was offering me a hand. He said that in the second email – that in some lives, we offer a hand up to someone, and that in other lives, it may be the other way around and we may need a hand up. Here was a hand. It was up to me to take it or not, and either way, he was a friend. It was like a light had appeared at the end of this dark tunnel I found myself in. I printed out the contract. I sat with it in my hands like a sacred gift. I signed it with my purple pen knowing that my life was changed.

It was only a day or two later when I had contact from May, Michael's spiritual sister and old friend, and now, my friend whom I see almost every day.

About 2 years after that, I came to Perth to live near to Michael. I came to attend classes and to learn from him, to raise my son amidst May's kid's classes, and to follow my heart's knowing in a place where I am truly supported.

I tried to recall where I had met May before and was sure that she was an old friend. Then her daughter found a photo taken by her mother, at the snowline at the base of Mount Shasta. She pointed out that I was in the photo. May and I were shocked. How was this possible? I scanned the photo. Yes, that was my jacket, I remembered standing up there in the icy wind, joining a group photo as I looked out over the world from that snowy energy vortex, wondering about my life. Little did I know, May was that woman I kept running into! That event was part of the pathway to being here, now, taking up my place, living and learning from Michael, his wife Segolene, and their co-facilitator, Amy. There is no place I would rather be.

The following twenty years have been an incremental extraction of my psyche from a most formidable fairytale life, re-directing my consciousness to, as Michael has often said, 'Stop imagining and experience the real.'

Over the years, and especially in the beginning, my fairytale pursuits have sometimes spilled over to my relationship with Michael. I was so deeply entrenched in my reality that I suppose an inevitable side effect of extracting myself, awakening from my delusions, and clearing through my unresolved issues, was that I projected some of my reality at the greatest and clearest source of love in my life – Michael. Whenever I got my wires crossed, confusing the great love that I felt for human sentimentality or sexual desire, Michael would respond with compassion, coupled with very stark, strong and unwavering boundaries.

Michael not only maintains an incredibly high standard of ethics, but he also simply is not tempted by the things that other people are. He doesn't need to control any simmering urges – he simply does not have those urges. He is not holding back a tidal wave of lust or sentimental imaginings –

he has moved beyond such things, refining his character and raising the vibration of all his bodies so that they are faithful servants and representatives of his inner reality. Michael teaches self-mastery and synthesis, and he emphasises the importance of grounding higher energy here, in the body, so that the body can be transformed. He does not struggle with the things that his students struggle with, and so he is able to act as a clear barometer and mirror for us, unwavering and clear.

Over the years, whenever I have struggled with my sexual nature and directed those desires Michael's way, he has simply said, 'No, absolutely not', and then he has helped me to further work on healing the part of me which confuses love with sex, teaching me that unconditional love does not seek to own or to possess – unconditional love is given freely, without expectation. Love is what binds and fuels all of life. It is the force which runs through all things, as natural as the sun and the trees and the soil. Love does not need to be "done"; it simply is.

Michael has explained that any teacher who abuses their position and becomes sexually involved with a student is committing an act which is akin to spiritual paedophilia. In such a relationship, there is no equality. The student will always be looking up to the teacher, and the student will tend to follow the teacher's lead. How can any student, who is so deeply impacted in this way, ever give proper consent?

He also explains that it is abhorrent and abusive behaviour for a teacher to take advantage of a student's spiritual awakening. With spiritual awakening comes a great influx and down-pouring of energy, as well as an opening of the chakras. This energy and this opening are for the student – it is a precious and wondrous occurrence, and the energy is intended to be used for the student's own revelation, growth, and evolution. It is a deeply personal experience, one which is occurring between the student and Life Itself, and it is not to be meddled with.

A teacher who takes advantage of this energy and this opening is effectively stealing energy and using it to make themselves feel a certain way – special, important or significant as they "enable the healing of the goddess" (I came across this particular New Age claim a lot, prior to working with Michael). To get high on energy which is intended to activate and awaken another is to commit an evolutionary crime, and such "teachers" are not teachers at all – they are very defective energetic parasites, driven and motivated by their own low self-worth and lack of integration.

This has been priceless learning from Michael, and to have him hold me in a clear, steady and non-judgemental space while I have floundered my way through my confusion has changed me as a human and as a soul, altering the course of my life now, and all future lives to come.

This process has involved learning discernment, often the hard way. Having told myself that everyone and everything is love, seeing only what I wanted to see, protecting myself from seeing my own monsters and those in others, I was ill equipped to face reality. I don't know how I could have gotten through that delusion without learning how to tell the difference between what was my stuff and how to clear it, and what was not my stuff and how to stop trying to process that.

One of the major foundational tools that got me on track was the energetic hygiene process that was presented from the first early days of the Lightworker's program. Over the years, energetic hygiene has not waned in importance.

Michael held weekly classes and retreats where we would sometimes hear anecdotes and stories, and it would slowly dawn on me, over time, that every resource we have was born of his blood, sweat and tears in a major way. It was all his life experience, his lives and his works as a soul, poured into all these maps, to help anyone who had the eyes to see, the ears to hear, and the heart to recognise that he had found a way through the labyrinth. He had thoroughly fleshed out the path that he had trodden, so as to make the process learnable and reproducible. Like runway lights at the airport, Micheal, getting around in his humble way, was very busy forging ahead, but his love was also leaving a very bright, unmistakable way forward for those who were coming after.

These may be ancient teachings, but they have been updated to be relevant to the times we live in. And oh, what times we live in. Micheal carved a path himself, with his own experience teaching him, listening to the knowing that guided him through, gathering empirical evidence of what worked and what did not. He seems to have reviewed and refined and learned and reverse engineered and consolidated every drop of the life that he has wisely lived. He has shared his findings, and others have tried it and gotten results.

I was not around when these tools were originally created. They feel as ancient as the commandments. But I do know that Michael has studied far and wide, involving himself with the adepts, the Masters, theology, and ancient teachings throughout history, all of which he sifts through to extract the jewels of truth. The magic of energy hygiene is not a quick fix, a one-weekend-to-awakening thing. Working with this tool is to refine, to clarify, to purify and drop the judgment in every moment. It is not a matter of reading affirmations, though that is where I started. It has taken 20 years of persistent application (especially in the times of thick resistance) to penetrate some of the imprints and beliefs I have had. I am still learning to be a little less wrong every day.

This is one of the most beautiful gifts I have received from Michael. He is very enthusiastic about discovering things that might be "wrong". He says that, 'You can either be right all the time or you can realise God, but you can't do both'. You can only learn, only evolve, if you are wise enough to recognise the things that you don't already know. There are always things to learn, always way to improve, always greater experiences of love to expand into – there are always "wrong" things to discover and replace with more of the Truth. If we haven't realised to the attainment of God yet, then we must, of course, be wrong. This revelation was such a great relief to me. I don't have to strive to be right all the time. I can be here now, as I am, and humbly surrender all the daily wrongness onto the refiner's fire, and relinquish control over to love, to light, and to life itself.

This ability to grow my confront and to face my delusions, bringing deep acceptance and gratitude for the learning that my fantasy-chasing has brought me, has come about as a result of being held in beautifully orchestrated kindness, a consistent and unfathomably patient love, and exquisite confront from the heart of a one-of-a=kind "unicorn man"; my dear friend and teacher, Michael. The blessing of slaying my fairytale is that I get to truly ground and express love within a life that is alive.

Michael's commitment to life, to his family, and to all his students, radiates a true, selfless intimacy and a presence that is immune to fairytales. He has shared about his goal to be as bright as he can be, shining his light to help others find their way in the dark. It certainly worked for me. He makes me want to be better to myself, to the Earth, and to all of life.

There are endless stories, quotes and experiences that have been shared with us over this magical time since I met Michael. I remember the first retreat I attended, where I found that I was not capable of making a commitment for 5 hours, and here was Michael talking about a 500-year plan. It was so sensible and compelling, and I decided that I was all in! By that afternoon session, we were discussing a 5000-year plan, and I laughed to myself. I was suddenly leaping at the chance to commit to service for that long. I had not even dreamed that I could be this expansive and embrace time in this way.

One day, during that first Wesak in Perth in 2005, I learned how to love myself enough to commit to be a part of something bigger. I got to work and cleaned up my mirror significantly enough to catch a glimpse of how far there is still to go. I am eternally grateful to be making the journey alongside Michael, Segolene, Amy and my spiritual family.

Thank you for this opportunity to love.

STORY FOUR

~ ~ ~

I had come to the end of more than twenty-five years with a spiritual guru-based group where I was a devotee, practising meditation techniques for extended periods and also teaching meditation. Devotion to the guru was a culture I immersed myself in from the age of thirteen. The organisation, over time, was not sitting right for me. Over those years I had experienced highs, yet I had also experienced deep lows and fears, and all of that was confusing.

Recently learning of the alleged abuse, ethical breaches, and corruption in that group has caused me to feel dismay. After spending so many years in that group, lending it my energy and passing on its teachings, I can't help but feel somewhat responsible as I witness the harm which has been caused to those who I have cared for and loved, and for those whom the group has claimed to care for and love. This abuse of spiritual power is heart-wrenching, and I have personally witnessed the harm that it can cause.

It is heartening to have been studying with Michael King for over twenty years now and to be experiencing just how different an integrated teacher, and a group which is holding accountability to exacting standards, can be. With exposé after exposé of the inappropriate and unethical behaviours of teachers in the new age, religious, spiritual, yoga and meditation worlds happening, Michael, his wife Segolene, and their co-facilitator Amy, are a breath of truly fresh spiritual air. And they all work hard for it. Michael is a unicorn man, an initiate and a mouthpiece for, and in service to, greater and more loving energies and this beautiful planet.

No grandstanding or outlandish claims, no fancy name or title, no special clothes or hats (well, actually, over the years I have seen him dress up in costumes and funny hats, up on the speaking stage, to humorously show its folly), and no empire building. Michael is authentic. When the humble residential retreat centre opened its doors for the first in-house retreat, I had the idea for a ribbon cutting and I asked Michael about it. He simply said no. There is no pomp and circumstance. It is all real and true, and getting on with, preparing for, and enjoying service.

After I left the guru-based group, I was unsure of what to do next. Coming out of a yoga class one Saturday morning in Melbourne, I picked up a new age paper from the stand. As a passenger on the drive home, I was flicking through the pages feeling sceptical of the myriads of spiritual offerings and weekend workshops. One advertisement for an event, with a photo of Michael King, caught my attention. I thought, 'he looks unusual, and I want to contact him.'

Michael answered when I phoned a couple of days later. I rambled about my experiences and what I was looking for. He gave me the location, time, and cost for his classes, and said, 'Come along and see if it resonates', and hung up. That was twenty-two years ago.

An early workshop I attended with Michael was in a full room, and he was out the front teaching and swearing. I was just a little more confused than self-righteous when I questioned him, privately, telling him that I thought it was wrong for spiritual teachers to swear. This was a "do not put me on a pedestal" moment, as he encouraged me to see some of my own dogmatic assertions and assumptions. With Michael, there is no hint of "holier than thou". There is no superiority, and there are no attempts to be viewed as anything righteous or unattainable. He is genuine, honest and authentic.

Michael always encourages his students not to become devoted to him; not to hold him up and praise him as some external and impossible-to-reach God. He is intentionally very normal, even when offering us extraordinary insight into rather unusual and multidimensional realities. He discourages hero-worship, encouraging integration and actualisation instead. Bring it through, and simply be it.

At another workshop, Michael talked about the tendency of the fear-based negative ego to see-saw between inferiority and superiority. He spoke about calm assurance and a solid self-esteem as being the remedy for this, replacing the highs and lows of external dependency with an experience of harmony and equanimity. It was a relief to hear my own concerning experiences explained so simply, and to perceive of a path to transcend this dynamic.

Michael freely shares his own life learnings and inner experiences, offering guidance for integrated heart-mastery to his students in classes, in forums, in passing, and on retreats. From the multi-dimensional to the basic, and including (not so common) commonsense for daily life, Michael generously embodies and offers it all. If I had of completely and consistently applied everything that Michael recommended, I would now be in a far greater state of self-mastery than I am. Despite not always being a model student, Michael's love and encouragement is always consistent.

Over all the years I have known him, his commitment and service to higher love stands out, uncompromising. Also his kindness and his creativity in sharing the simple (though not always easy) foundations of the alchemical way of heart-mastery, over and over.

Michael does not believe in luck – he shows what it is like to live a life of service where choices are made in order to serve a higher purpose, and he teaches the simplicity of accepting that all choices have consequences. He empowers us to understand that we are the creators of our own realities.

By embracing trials and accepting responsibility, Michael has worked for every step of his attainment, and he teaches his students to do the same. Every experience is an opportunity to learn, to grow, to love a little bit more, and to ground and express self-mastery.

Michael has an engineer's mind. He loves designing, process engineering and reverse engineering, both physically and energetically, and I have been a beneficiary of this alchemy. He encourages his students to perceive of their potential, and then he encourages them along a roadmap which will bring about the actualisation of that potential. With his particular outlook, he can see what needs to be integrated, transcended, healed, transformed and realised in order for certain outcomes to be achieved.

The expansiveness of the higher love that I have experienced in Michael's processes has been tremendous. However, the human interactions have been richer for me because it has taught me that they are not separate – that true spirituality is lived and expressed in the human life, even through the most normal or mundane of tasks.

In the early days, Michael offered individual insight readings, and after I had signed up to his life coaching program, I booked a reading at his home. His wife welcomed me and showed me downstairs to his office. As I entered, there was a sliding glass door open to the outside garden. Near Michael, on the floor, stood a magpie. Michael said to the magpie, 'Mate, I've got something on now', and the magpie walked out the door as I sat down.

Michael sat quietly across from me. He was scanning my energy quotients (for example, love, light, transcension of negative ego, inner teamwork) from the previous months on the coaching program, and all seemed on a progressing track. Then he paused and sad, 'About two weeks ago your energy took a big dip. If you can feel into what was going on for you then, it might give you good insight.' I reflected over that period, and nothing came to mind, so I pulled my diary out from my bag and flipped through the days and my activities. Then it jumped out. I had been trying to get (i.e. coerce) my husband to attend a workshop of Michael's over this period. I thought it would be good for him, and I assumed that I knew what was right for him. At first, I was "sweetly" encouraging, and then I switched to being "sweetly" manipulative.

My husband did end up coming along, very patiently, and I thought I had a win! Self-righteousness and deciding what others needed ran deep for me, and by seeing this reflected in my energy signature over this period, Michael showed me the way of insight. I was able to have this self-discovery, which was a sobering win, and it was refreshing to feel that there was no judgment on Michael's part. It was early days of being a devotee to the truth – of truly wanting to know the truth, no matter what – and I was just beginning the process of developing my own self-esteem and self-respect, which involved clearing my character flaws.

Michael keeps student numbers low enough to ensure that he can fulfil his duty of care for them all. He has a very different approach than other spiritual teachers I have known – rather than gathering a large and dependent flock of followers around him, Michael understands the importance of personal care. With each individual's evolutionary journey being different, and with a goal and a genuine desire to teach self-mastery and sovereignty (rather than setting himself up as a permanent and unattainable intermediary between his students and God), Michael seeks to find ways to make the process of actualisation attainable. If his students numbered in the thousands, how could he possibly tend to each of them?

Michael has witnessed how easily and how quickly spiritual groups and teachers can become corrupt, and so he sets very high standards of psychological and spiritual clarity. He seeks to build a team around him who uphold his high level of ethics and insight, personally training them to become clear mirrors, mentors and facilitators, and he only allows his student body to grow as his team, which he oversees, becomes ready.

Once, when I had come over from the USA to attend a spiritual function which was being hosted by Michael, I stayed with him and his wife. While I was there, I took a train trip into Melbourne to visit friends for a couple of nights. My sense of entitlement preceded me (the self-righteousness thread went deep) when I assumed and expected that Michael, or his wife, would collect me on my return, without my even asking them. Confused, I caught buses and walked back to the house in unusually hot weather, carrying my bag. Far from being disregarding or inconsiderate, this was another deliberate lesson about humility and self-responsibility. Michael and his wife warmly welcomed me home, pleased to see me, and helped me to understand that of course they would have been happy to collect me from the train station, if only I had asked.

I was still relatively fresh from living and functioning as a member of a co-dependent spiritual community. My years in the ashram had left me a bit clueless about normal human life and how to take responsibility for myself. I wasn't used to making my own decisions, and I certainly wasn't used to being empowered to take care of myself and my own needs.

This was essential learning and a priceless gift from Michael – he helped me to be able to navigate in the world again; sovereign, directing my own life, and taking responsibility for the consequences of my choices (or non-choices).

During another stay, I was up early. The house was quiet, and there had been a storm in the night. I looked out the kitchen window and a big branch had broken off a gum tree right outside. I could see that Michael had been up during the night to wrap its wound. I was deeply moved by this innocent display of care.

At the end of this trip, I was in the driveway preparing to leave for the journey back to the USA. In the last moments, Michael appeared, eyes blinking in the light, and said goodbye, giving me a hug. He said, 'Ah, the tyranny of distance.' He also shares with his students, 'I am only ever a thought away.' I have known and felt this to be true.

Channelling was still new to me. I had seen and heard many spiritual teachers channelling and it was often quite a sensational show. At times, I found it hard to tell when Michael was channelling and when he was, well, Michael. Now, it does not matter. He often shares it is not about the messenger; it is about the message. He cautions his students about putting on a "show" or about being the "show". He also teaches that the clarity and the purity of both the source and the messenger are key.

At another ascension event that he hosted, I was standing with other students near to him at the desk where he was mixing and managing the stage sound. A popular and charismatic new age teacher was on stage and Michael quietly leaned over and shared, 'When he thinks he is channelling he is not, and when he thinks he is not, he is.' This was a practical lesson in discernment and about the need to get out of the way for the flow of spiritual energy. You can't "do" channelling – you must surrender yourself to the channel so that energy can ground and express through you.

After another event, the new age circuit presenters and musicians, who had come from the USA, gathered in Michael's loungeroom. On this occasion, with guests staying, my bed was in a corner of the spacious loungeroom. It had been a long weekend and evening, and I had slipped over to lie on my bed as Michael was spending time with the guests. I watched as Michael shape shifted and I saw his face and energy change, like film frames, one life after the other. It is very unusual to see Michael openly display these kinds of abilities.

Michael has repeatedly emphasised that the most important thing is to ground and express love, sharing that the overt display of spiritual gifts is really just art for art's sake. 'What does that have to do with grounding and expressing love?' is a question that we regularly hear him ask his students. Spiritual gifts should only be displayed as a way of creating an outcome of love. I realised that Michael was communicating with his guests in a way which they would actually pay attention to. Far from being receptive to his usual and preferred down-to-earth way of communicating, he realised that his guests were most open to spiritual messages and love if they were accompanied by a certain level of pomp which they, as a result of their own spiritual training, considered to be impressive. I learned that Michael is not rigid – not set in his ways – and that his commitment to create outcomes of love is absolute, taking on a great many guises.

When returning from the USA to live in Australia, we travelled via England, where Michael was also visiting. One of Michael's students, who was based in the UK, had organised a tour of sacred sites for a coach full of participants. We visited locations on the 'All Souls' coach (yes, that was the real name) including the Avebury Standing

Stones, Stonehenge, crop circles, old forests, Glastonbury, and the Tor. At most sites, Michael ran a meditative process with those of us on the tour.

For me, the most heartfelt experience from that time was beneath Westminster in Winston Churchill's war rooms. Michael, his wife, and my husband and I, toured the war rooms which were in use twenty-four hours a day from 1939 until 1945. Coming back out after a couple of hours or more, we headed off in different directions for the rest of the afternoon. I cried for the two and a half miles walking back to our accommodation, feeling what had occurred in those years. The course of humanity's future had been redirected from those rooms, and I felt the significance of that.

For over eight years, Michael, his wife, and my husband and I, were partners in a women's health club franchise. Once I was back in Australia and the clubs were operational, we had regular dinner meetings to report about the business. Both men had their own daily jobs so we, the wives, took care of the day-to-day business operations and membership. Michael was always very encouraging about our abilities.

To go from meditating a lot to being instrumental in running five businesses was a notable change for me. One day I was up a ladder cleaning light fittings in preparation for opening one of our clubs, and I was also listening to one of the ascension CD resources Michael had recorded for his students. Michael came by to check in and I was listening to his recorded process intently through my earphones. I did not take my earphones off – I never let anyone interrupt my Michael processes, not even him. Michael spoke loudly, quizzically, 'But I am right here', he said.

I found this exchange funny, and it also helped me to see how I still had a tendency to segregate my spiritual life from my human life. My preference was still to have my head in the clouds, prioritising my spiritual practices over being present and attentive in my human life, benefiting from on-the-ground lessons and experiences. This has been, and continues to be, a huge learning curve for me. Spirituality is not something that you do instead of living – the two should dance together, supporting and encouraging refinement and actualisation in each other.

Sometime later, I was selling part of the business on. After signing a binding contract, the woman who was purchasing part of the business went into fear and had a huge emotional reaction. Witnessing her reaction, I conceded to let her out of the deal and released her from the contract. When I told Michael, he said that he could not be involved in my decision to support her as she chose fear. He stood for love. I could feel the love that Michael had for this woman – he genuinely desired for her to succeed, and I could feel how he naturally sought to champion her in any way that he could. The clarity of his love helped me to see that, by encouraging her to give in to her fears instead of encouraging her and supporting her as she faced them, I had thwarted her opportunity to step up, to learn and to grow.

This was a valuable lesson for me. I learned how easy it could be to interfere in the growth, the evolution, and the chosen learning of other people. I also learned that love is not sentimental – it is kind, and it is compassionate, but love is always seeking to serve evolution. Love always considers the bigger picture and the intention of the soul. Love always works for the highest good of all concerned, to ultimately bring about outcomes of more love.

Just the other night, after Michael's weekly class finished, I was walking behind him and his daughter as they started their walk home. It was dark, a sliver of a moon in the sky, and she said, 'I do not have a torch or my phone'. Michael replied, 'We could practise our sensing and night-seeing to make our way in the dark.' I chimed in, 'That is fun.'

Michael kept walking and said, over his shoulder, 'That *is* fun.'

Simple as it might seem, this little comment from Michael is significant – however difficult the journey may sometimes appear, and however much it may sometimes feel as though we are pressing forward, blindly searching for our way home in the darkness, we must remember to seek out sources of light, and to not to take ourselves too seriously.

Life is exploring itself through us, and we are exploring ourselves through life. This is a wondrous adventure that we are all on together. Too often, we forget the magic and the joy; we forget to let ourselves experience the awe and the natural wonder of exploring and practicing our sensing and our night-seeing as we make our way in the apparent darkness.

I have learned that, with a light which shines as brightly as Michael does, we are never truly in darkness and the journey really *is* fun.

STORY FIVE

~~~

I recall first finding Michael and Cosmosis® in 2002 - about 22 years ago now. I had been putting it out to the universe, seriously asking for about six months or more, night and morning, for my teacher to come into my life. After much active searching, I finally found what I had been seeking. I am chagrined to acknowledge that I was fairly sceptical at first, looking for cracks in some sort of façade that I was certain must be there. Sceptical or not however, at this point I decided to participate in one of the weekly teleclasses, but with low expectations. Most of what was available was unimpressive and not really worth going back for a deeper dive, so there wasn't a lot of enthusiasm on my part.

I will, for the record, point out that I was happy with my life back then. I had easy work that was mostly enjoyable, I played sports, had a circle of friends, went on holidays, went to the theatre, and so forth. But there was something missing. I didn't know what it was, but I was at a moment in time where I felt that there must be more to life than this. Everything seemed a little hollow, and so the search had begun in earnest.

As stated, I was pretty sceptical and mistrusting, but deciding to attend that first tele class was a turning point for me. Unfortunately, I am unable to recall the subject of that class, but I know how it made me feel; how Michael made me feel. I recall that it gave much to ponder. Things I had sensed for myself but had never voiced to anyone before… things I only half-knew… things I felt but wasn't yet aware of… things I didn't yet know… all this and more came tumbling into my awareness and settled there for the long haul.

Something in Michael's words – no – it was something in how he WAS that drew me. Down-to-earth. Matter of fact. He presented these concepts in a way that was simple, understandable, yet profoundly deep and moving. I came away somehow changed, without really understanding how. This new feeling stayed with me all week. My worldview had been challenged, and something in me was shifting. I wanted more, so the following week I fronted up again, ready to learn, but still not quite trusting what I felt.

I attended each week, looking forward to the class and to the connection I felt with this stranger. Week after week I was astonished at how the discourses were totally applicable to what was happening in my life, right then and there, on the ground. I was the primary carer for my elderly parents, working as an actor, and working nights at a local restaurant. I was terribly caught up in gossip and what other people thought of me. I would turn myself inside out to try and please everyone.

I remember one of the first things I heard Michael share was that, 'what other people think of us is none of our business'. What? I had never heard that before. I sat there, stunned, as it sank right into my core. Was I allowed to not mind what other people said, or did, or believed? Really? It rocked my world, and I spent that week deeply pondering this. Suddenly I heard this maxim being said in the world around me. How could I have never heard this before? I began paying attention to my actions, my motives, and the expected reactions that others wanted from me.

Week after week, I implemented and practiced the simple yet profound teachings of this man. I found my world and my perceptions shifting bit by bit.

This man spoke of unconditional love, compassion, and kindness. He spoke of truth, integrity, and ethics. He spoke of unity and harmony, oneness and humility. These were pretty big concepts to be espousing. Did he walk the talk? Over the years of being privileged to observe his actions firsthand, I can unequivocally say that yes, Michael is a man of his word. It's not often that you find someone who says what he means and means what he says.

If something is not in alignment with the highest outcome for all concerned, Michael will call it out and refuse to be a part of whatever is out of step with what is called for ethically, regardless of who or what that might be. From what I have observed, everything he does is for the upliftment of everything on this planet. This doesn't mean he is easy to push around. Quite the contrary. He is steadfast in his commitment to love and to all that is of benefit to humanity and the planet – to all that is sacred – and he is willing to draw a very firm line in the sand which will not be crossed if it's about anything less than unconditional love.

In my early encounters with the teachings, I learned the importance of bringing everything back to myself, moving away from being a victim of circumstance, and embracing a place of truth where I could acknowledge my part in what was playing out. We cannot control the world, but we can control our responses to the people and events of our lives. I came to learn that I am enough and that, rather than finding my worth in the thoughts and projections of others, I am okay in who I am.

Judgement was a big part of my life. I loved to judge, 'I deem this to be good, and I deem that to be bad!' It felt powerful and righteous. But I came to feel how it was actually keeping me locked in that cycle of overly caring about the opinions of others. Frankly, it was exhausting and costing me my peace. However, at the time, I was still unconscious of much of this. I had to learn to walk before I could run. I needed to disentangle myself from the unhelpful patterns I had become enmeshed with. With Michael walking beside me, championing me, I knew I could do it.

I began applying the foundational teachings, such as cord clearing, energetic cleansing, energetic protection, and the like, and found that the results spoke for themselves; my life seemed to be changing for the better. I found deeper purpose and meaning. I began to feel lighter and happier than I had before. I had spent my life living under a well-hidden cloud of depression – living a façade of cheeriness to keep the people around me happy, all while hiding the sadness that even I was unable to see or feel. As I listened to this very natural Aussie who spoke in a way which was real and not the "hype" I had experienced from other so-called spiritual teachers, Michael's discourses became the highlight of my week.

When I was invited to attend a workshop in Melbourne, for that was where he was living at the time, I jumped at the chance to go and "feel" this teacher "in person". I believed, at the time, that I had a good b/s barometer, and that I would find the so-called "cracks".

Michael had been holding classes and workshops there for some time and had a group of earnest students, many of whom were gathered for this workshop. I sat myself in the second row, near the end so that I could hide in plain sight and observe in order to gauge the mettle of this man.

Sitting in front of me was one of his more vocal students who argued with him, interrupted him, and who, in my mind, made quite a nuisance of themselves. I was at the point of considering something quite unspiritual at the time, yet this gentle man simply moved to stand in front of this person and ignored, or responded, as required, with only kindness and love shining from his countenance. There was never even a shred of impatience or judgement.

At first, I was incredulous. How could he stand this? How could this poor behaviour be so indulged? Why did he not cut this person off? Why were they not torn down, or at the very least put firmly in their place? Reviewing such thoughts now, many years later, I understand the compassion and tolerance inherent in the teachings, as well as in the teacher. However, at the time I was at the start of my journey, and I had a long way to travel before I learned true patience, tolerance, and kindness.

So, in observing this teacher and his interactions with this student, I was struck by his total lack of judgement. I reflected, as I sat with my arms folded, squinting at Michael, looking for the cracks, that if this vociferous and annoying student had not been there, right in front of me, I would not have been afforded such a wonderful opportunity to observe this initiate in action in real time. In fact, I would go so far as to say that I became hugely grateful towards that difficult student, for without such a tangible and felt experience of utter non-judgement, patience, and unconditional love, I would not be, still to this day, a student and follower of this man.

And, as if by magic, that student seated in front of me suddenly no longer annoyed me. Something inside me changed in that moment. I wanted to learn how to love like that, how to be so patient and kind. I wanted to learn from this man. I wanted to follow these teachings, and I wanted to become a student in this group. I was still sceptical, but I was committed to something that was on offer there that day.

Now, some 22 years later, reflecting on the time spent learning from this man, I feel how far I've travelled, and how much more is available for me to travel. It hasn't always been easy or smooth. I've resisted and fought and argued. I've sulked and squirmed and projected. I've been sure that I've been hard done-by in many moments, and, to the casual observer, this may have seemed the case. However, as I look back now, I see the perfection of the lessons I was learning at the time. I also feel the self-mastery of my teacher and the way he held the mirror steady for me.

You see, I had grown up in the 50's and 60's, when children were treated somewhat differently from how they are treated today. In addition to this, I had a somewhat self-absorbed mother and an enabling father, both of whom taught me that love was purely transactional, something to be avoided at all costs, and that people are never real and are always putting on an act. Hence, I was very dubious of Michael and what he had to say for many years. Yet, my heart felt the veracity of what was shared with us. There was something that kept me coming back and very slowly opening up in spite of my egoic misgivings. Slowly but surely, I was growing and changing for the better.

In that workshop I learned the finer details of what became known as "Energetic Hygiene" and the importance of it becoming a daily practice. I learned how one becomes corded or tied to others energetically. I could feel how entangled my whole family and all my friends were, and recognised how this was not healthy for any of us as it kept us impacted by events and the vagaries of others, rather than being empowered to be at cause in our lives. I learned how to clear these cords, how to clear negativity from my energy field, and how to protect it. These are basic tools that can be used by anyone – they are simple and effective – but I had to learn to apply them consistently and consciously, over and over!

I have to say, however, that not everyone was happy at losing their free access to my time and energy. In fact, it caused quite a bit of bother as I disentangled myself from the intricacies of the web I had woven myself into. I wouldn't have been able to stick with it had it not been for the gentle and loving encouragement from my teacher. He was with me every step of the way, showing me how to disengage myself gracefully without causing too much ruckus or negativity from those around me, and how to do it with love and compassion, as I was the one who was changing the rules of the game. I also saw how, by disentangling myself and having clear boundaries in place, I became more able to unconditionally love and altruistically engage with the people in my life. Rather than robbing me of my relationships, my new-found boundaries caused my relationships to become more genuine, wholesome and rewarding for everyone involved.

There were times when my actions and choices did cause reactions in others, but I was gently encouraged to reflect and to find where I had perhaps come from a place of judgement or self-righteousness, where I had been mean and had wanted "my" way, and how it might have been different had I made the same choice but from a kinder or more loving space. There was never any judgement on Michael's part, only kindness and love.

It took quite a bit of work to start shifting this pattern, and the work continues as the lines get finer and finer, but my world began changing that day when I made my commitment to walk this path with Michael by my side, and it continues to change for the better. While the lessons may seem simplistic on the outside, there is the undercurrent of unconditional acceptance and unconditional love which underpins the teachings and allows them to seep into my bones, into my very core. It is a challenging task to stop running, turning, instead, to face one's "unpretty" bits.

And so, after attending that fateful workshop where I came face-to-face with this initiate, for that is what he is in every sense to me, I felt the call and applied to become a serious student. It was at the end of November in 2002, and I recall standing in the hallway talking to Michael about it. As the primary carer for my parents, and as we were travelling overseas to visit my sister for Christmas, I was considering whether to start now or when I returned. Michael didn't mind but he helped me to ponder the benefits of travelling with the support of Cosmosis® rather than losing the current momentum I had built from attending classes and now the workshop.

I wanted time to think about this and to speak with my family about my time commitments to the work while also travelling and caring for them. His gentle and benevolent countenance stayed with me as I travelled back to Sydney, reflecting on how to frame this new way that I wanted to live and be in the world, while still fulfilling my commitments to my responsibilities. I knew I wanted this with all my heart and soul, and I didn't want to lose the flow of what was opening for me. It was a choiceless choice, but I wanted to feel that I had given it enough consideration. This was probably unnecessary, but at the time I was still disentangling myself from caring too much about the opinions of others.

Suffice it to say that by the time I had travelled back to Sydney I had made up my mind to join the programme immediately. Now, it was just a matter of sharing that news with my family in a way which wouldn't cause them anxiety, rather that they would be as happy as I was.

And, as a side note, I was very glad of the support and love I received while travelling. Once a student has connected with their teacher and is committed to the practices, it matters not if they are in the physical presence of each other or if they are physically far apart. I knew and felt Michael's love and support, not just when in meditation or while doing the daily practices, but constantly. His presence was tangible, walking alongside me in every moment. I reflected at the end of each day whether it had been smooth or otherwise, what the events of the day had taught me, and how I could have done it better. I felt the ever-gentle, ever-loving presence of Michael guiding, teaching, and showing me the way. Even when I had forgotten him in the moment, he had never forgotten me.

There are so many stand-out instances to relate, and I hope some of these small moments help to paint a picture of how my life has turned around for the better.

Another moment etched into my memory occurred during a retreat which Michael was facilitating. For the purpose of teaching, he had asked one of the students to relate a horrific event (from which this person had healed so much under Michael's guidance, that it did not even cause them the slightest pain to retell it). The student was happy to share and stood in front of us, retelling simply the facts – no embellishments or emotions – just what happened. There was hardly a dry eye in the room. When the student resumed their seat, and people had dried their eyes and blown their noses, Michael looked at us with kind and loving eyes, and admonished us sternly.

'Who had found that hard and cried?', he asked. Most of us raised our hands for we cared about our fellow student and could well sympathise with them, thinking how we might feel if it were us. But far from our expressions of care and concern being an expression of love, we were sternly, yet lovingly, shown the potential harm we could cause through our judgements and beliefs. We had all just cast our friend as a victim. That was not love. Energy follows thought and we, en masse, had felt sorry for this person, effectively disempowering them, and regarding them as a victim. Thus, we had added to the burden of what had occurred almost as much as the original perpetrator.

I was aghast! I immediately saw how this perpetuates events, keeping them stuck to a person, not allowing them to grow beyond the confines of happenstance. It had such a profound effect on me. Immediately I could review my life and see how this was a tool which was used by my family for grabbing energy, for keeping control of people or things, and for gaining advantage over others. I felt ashamed that I had played this game, albeit unconsciously thus far, but now it was time to change.

It isn't easy to transform oneself. It takes considerable focus and attention to detail. One has to want to change, but that wanting isn't really enough. Michael would often talk to us about intention, persistence, and action. There is a lot of talk about the power of intention, however, he shared with us, just simply intending something does not create the change we wish to see in the world. We must embody that change, heart and soul. To create change we must be willing AND able.

Sometimes we are willing, but not able. Sometimes we are able, but not willing.

True change requires the presence of both. Our patterns and programs that have guided our behaviour may have helped us to cope in this often-uncaring world. They may have helped us to survive, but mere survival is not enough if we want to evolve. I have to say, part of me was very much on board for change, but part of me certainly wasn't and this part would burst forth in moments, causing me to cringe at my behaviour, and leaving me wanting to hide away in my embarrassment. Michael would patiently share that judging ourselves only keeps the energy stuck to us, as, essentially, we are feeding energy to what we do not desire and turning away from the love which would help us, in that moment, to transcend the pattern.

This was one of my toughest habits to break, and one that would take me a long time to clear. Having grown up in an era of punishment, and having experienced much criticism, my lenses were firmly fixed on my belief that everyone, no matter what they say, is secretly judging and criticising you - always. For many years I tried to hide this belief, trying to please and appease, trying so hard to be "spiritual" and a "good girl", but I was squirming on the inside, wracked with the pain of constant judgement, stubbornly believing that my kind and loving mentors must be judging me even more than I was judging myself.

I look back now and realise that I was only ever treated with genuine care, kindness, and unconditional positive regard. Sometimes the love was a tough love hammer where my fear-fuelled behaviours were uncomfortably highlighted, whilst at other times the love was a shoulder to cry on. Michael does not play games or manipulate. He is not interested in appeasing my ego. Sometimes, I am sure, it was very uncomfortable as I threw my projections at him while he valiantly worked to help me notice and clear something which was holding me back.

His interest is always in supporting me, as a spiritual being, to evolve. Always, he works in service of his students' spiritual growth. This is his profound gift to us. He encourages our evolution as the souls that we are, which, in turn, helps us to become better humans.

His overarching goal is for us to become fully present to our spiritual selves and to self-actualise, right here, right now – not by blissing off or by spacing out into higher dimensions or planes of existence, but by living and enjoying our lives as spirit clothed in human form – exuding love, gratitude, compassion, and wisdom in as many moments as we can.

Over the years I have consistently and diligently applied the teachings, often feeling like nothing was happening, but always being encouraged by Michael, his wife Segolene, and Amy, the other core Cosmosis® facilitator and mentor. It is a bit like learning a musical instrument – you do the five-finger exercises, and hope that one day you will be able to put it all together and play music. Michael and his team simply held me in a space of love as I flailed about with my five-finger exercises for all those years, until I was finally able to hold myself and put the work into practice. However much it may have felt like nothing was happening, the fruits of transformation that I now experience are evidence to the contrary. This stuff works.

Love, as Michael teaches us, is not simply an emotional opinion – it is a measurable force that serves the growth and upliftment of our higher selves.

His work, and our work together, has been beyond valuable for me.

I will end this chapter with the most recent experience of Michael and his core team's love and care.

Fifteen months ago, I was struck down with a massive bleed on the brain from a previously undiagnosed congenital malformation in the veins in my cerebellum. I spent over two months in the stroke ward of a hospital, and then 13 months in rehab as I worked to regain function. I was so loved and supported through this gruelling experience, and in spite of still being somewhat physically disabled, I am left with a deep feeling of gratitude and joy at the many gifts this opportunity has afforded me.

Michael's presence was constant and tangible throughout, and continues to be. While I was in critical care, he worked with me at a soul level to help maximise the potential of the situation, staying in constant energetic communication with me. My human life was hanging in the balance, yet I know with certainty that my soul was being held and nurtured and cared for while every effort was being made to support my physical body in what was needed.

I continue to be grateful for this whole difficult experience, and that is because of Michael's teachings and his love. He has helped me to come through this ordeal with gratitude and grace. Because of the tools I've integrated, the attitudes I've developed, and the ongoing support I've received, I have the strength to approach each day with hope and thankfulness for what I can do, and not lament the things that I can no longer do. My life is rich beyond belief because of him and his core team. He has helped me return to work recently, and I am now once again attending live Cosmosis® classes and the shorter retreats with him.

I feel truly blessed to have Michael, Segolene, Amy, and the others of my spiritual family in my life. I now know and feel a much truer version of love, which is still growing and evolving.

With all my heart and Soul, I thank the day I met Michael again in this life.

STORY SIX

~~~

It was the spring of 2004 when I first crossed paths with Michael in this life. I was living in the Dandenongs at the time, and I was rushing down the hill to catch a train. I ran past some shops and, out of the corner of my eye, spotted some friends that I'd recently made, in a Thai restaurant. They'd been helping run some meditation and self-mastery classes that I'd been intermittently going along to. While attending the classes, I'd heard quite a lot about Michael, their teacher and mentor.

As I stepped into the restaurant and greeted my friends, I noticed another gentleman with them. Something in me knew that it was Michael. They were standing at the counter; clearly, they had ordered some take away and were waiting for it. Before being introduced to this gentleman, I started chatting and catching up with my friends. We talked briefly about what we'd been up to recently - just general chit chat - but while we were talking, my ability to actually follow the conversation in a coherent manner completely evaporated. This other gentleman's presence was emanating so strongly that I was finding it incredibly difficult to follow the thread of the conversation. I didn't want to be rude, so I asked them to repeat what they were talking about, but after a couple of attempts and, still finding that I could not follow what they were saying, they said it didn't really matter and introduced me.

'This is Michael.' I turned to face him and the powerful presence emanating from him grew in intensity. Only now it started to feel as though the whole room was being flooded with this powerfully loving presence; like an immense waterfall was pouring through the ceiling, filling up the room around me, as well as pouring into my crown chakra and flooding my entire being. The air felt thick and liquid (like moving through honey) and shimmered with potential.

As I greeted him and took in his presence, everything slowed down, and a profound timelessness opened up. We locked eyes, and I felt him looking deeply into me. But it was more than that; it felt like he was also looking right through me, as though he was seeing not just me in that moment, but a thousand past versions of myself standing behind me – his gaze felt that deep and unwavering.

The other thing that was clear to me was how deeply interested he was in the core truth of my being, in my heart of hearts, and not just what I was presenting with my personality. I'd always felt a deep well within me (within my heart and soul), though it was mostly overlooked by others or well hidden from them. Up until that point, people had only ever looked *at* me, or, if they had tried to look *into* me, it was with such shallowness. Yet here was someone who not only noticed the deep well within me, but he was looking further into me than I'd ever dared to look myself. I'd never had anyone be so actively and genuinely interested in my core being before.

What was also clear was that he took nothing personally from me and that he remained unaffected; no thought, word, or action of mine could lessen his unwavering curiosity and interest in me. This apparent contradiction struck a chord in my heart. How was this possible?

As I absorbed his presence, what also struck me was how grounded he was in his body, and yet there was an authentic nobility that radiated from his core and whole being. It brought to mind the phrase, 'Head in the Heavens, Feet on the Earth.' He felt so grounded and anchored into the Earth, as though he was buried to his waist - deeply rooted - which allowed him to grow up out of the Earth with grace, strength, and purpose. The juxtaposition of these two truths shook me, yet here he was, actually embodying them.

This is why I share this story: time and again, Michael reveals to me, and to all his students, the actual ***embodiment*** of profound spiritual principles and sacred qualities. He ***lives*** from this deep well of wisdom, not in fleeting or random moments, but as a constant presence. He does not merely touch on these truths in passing; he exemplifies them fully and continuously. This is why he is such a rare jewel in this world. He walks the talk, consistently and tirelessly uncovering fresh ways to express these insights, helping his students to cultivate our own understanding, as he fosters our evolution into more maturity and wisdom.

We didn't actually exchange many words that day; the experience was more of a deep inner communion. He told me to 'keep the faith', I said 'I will', and then I turned back to my friends, confessed to how amazing the energy was, how much I was blown away by the experience. We all laughed, and then I went and caught my train.

To some, this may sound like fantastical storytelling, a creative embellishment, or some exaggerated imaginings to convey a parable. But I assure you that this actually all happened - and I've had hundreds more amazing experiences with Michael throughout the years. I've been around lots of interesting people in my life. I've been in the close presence of spiritual leaders, philosophers, and intellectuals; seen them talk in person to small and large groups. I've been around world-class actors, singers, musicians, and artists; seen them at their most intimate and raw, and also strutting their stuff on stage. Within a limited bandwidth, a few of them are able to energetically hold something quite beautiful, striking, or tangible, and share that with people. But nothing and no-one has ever come close to what Michael is able to embody. It is the difference between experiencing a gentle babbling brook and then stumbling upon Niagara Falls. The experience of being around that, and learning from that, is truly life-changing and transformational.

To be frank, after that meeting, it took me a few years to pluck up the courage to start working with him and the Cosmosis® Mentoring Centre. It's not that I wasn't curious or interested in what they were doing, I was just scared of working with a group. I was an incredibly sensitive kid and didn't feel like I belonged anywhere. I had learnt from experience to be sceptical of groups. Up to that point, all my experiences of being in groups were…shall I politely say…less than ideal. My overwhelming experience was that the more people there were in any group, the more internal politics there were, and the more people's negative egos, games, masks, and dysfunctional role-playing flared up.

From family to high school, to drama school, to being immersed in the acting industry, I found it difficult, being buffeted around by all of those dysfunctional patterns, limitations, and conditions. I preferred to keep to myself, have a small circle of friends, and be a bit of a lone wolf; keeping one eye always on the exit, in case things got toxic and destructive. That was my initial, self-taught, and clumsy way of trying not to get bogged down in all the politics, egos, and games. Ultimately, it was just another coping mechanism (one of many) that needed to be healed and transcended.

Eventually, the pressing need to sort through my soul baggage (as well as the difficulty of trying to cope with my sensitivities in an overwhelming society) became greater than the fear of working with a group. I felt the deep calling to explore that ancient question, 'Who Am I?' I wanted to get to the heart of the matter and find out who I really was underneath everything. That is, after all, what drew me to acting in this life; the chance to explore all of these different characters and archetypes so I could delve deeper into my own humanity and soul, and then hopefully move audiences as I did so.

So, in March 2008, I dived in. Instantly, I knew it was the right decision. I had found my tribe!

Without a doubt, it was (and still is) one of the best decisions I've ever made. The experience has felt like a steady, progressive unfurling of awakening and coming home - to my Self, to God/Love, to the Planet, and to Life itself. It is a feeling of no longer needing to be a lone wolf, or trying to fit in, or fearing being cast out. I feel sucked into place, I am allowing myself again to co-create with life, and I am allowing life to flow through me. It is immensely sacred and dear to me to feel this reconnection taking root and flourishing; to be of use again to the evolutionary forces; to feel truly alive and to celebrate the gift of life in all its kaleidoscopic technicolour. I am profoundly grateful to all that Michael has taught and offered me.

That's not to say that the journey of healing my soul baggage has always been smooth sailing for me. Far from it, but I wouldn't want to be anywhere else. Learning from Michael, as he expertly guides me on this healing journey, is the opportunity and privilege, not just of this lifetime, but of many lifetimes.

I feel to share with you a little bit about the state I was in when I joined the Cosmosis® Mentoring Centre, so you can have a more tangible and grounded experience of my growth, and understand the profound effect and influence Michael has had on my life.

I grew up in a very strict and stressed household and then was sexually abused by a Scout leader in my teens. I shut down in a big way and kind of imploded. On the outside I seemed to be functioning reasonably okay, but internally I was very lost. I built up all these defenses and twisted coping mechanisms to try to prevent me from being trampled down by society or shoehorned into some mediocre mould of existence.

I'd been out of drama school for a few years and had some reasonable success in getting some acting roles, but it was haphazard, and every rejection cut me like a knife. I could feel the potential in me to be a great actor, to have a meaningful career, to live an expansive life, and to be of use to the greater good, but I felt so blocked and buried inside of me, that I could only access it in fleeting moments. And worst of all, it seemed like everyone else I met was incapable of recognising even a flicker of greatness within me, let alone being able to see it manifest. This stung so deeply, and I became tortured by it. I was desperate to prove people wrong (never a good motive) and was also frightened that I may be deluding myself. I was consumed with trying to hone my craft, trying to find my voice as an artist, and somehow discover success, but deep down I was really terrified that failure would haunt me forever and I would live a mediocre life.

I explored so many experiences to try and reawaken myself but they were all dead-ends. I felt so shut down. I had lost the delicate precision in my being, the fine threads of articulation in my expression. It was like trying to play the guitar with two hammers instead of two hands. I felt stunted, blunt, numb, and shackled physically, emotionally, mentally, and spiritually.

This was the state I was in when I joined the Cosmosis® Mentoring Centre. Not a simple case. I was quite battered and bruised.

Michael assigned me a mentor to work with and started me on the Energy Hygiene course. It involved a lot of self-introspection and exploration to do with my boundaries, and how to clear and align my energy. Had these experiences been my only encounters in the group, they alone would have been profoundly transformative, instilling life skills and insights that I use daily and will use forever more. Working with boundaries, energetic clearing, and energetic integrity has been a major lesson for me. My life is vastly different from working with these tools.

Over the weeks and months, I practiced daily disciplines, spiritual exercises, and participated in weekly calls that he and the core team set out for me, which gave me much needed support, and something profoundly wise and true to align to. Bit by bit, these skills helped me to unplug myself and undo a lot of the learning and faulty programming that I'd taken on in my upbringing.

One of these practices involves listening to a discourse or meditation process, which has been recorded on CD, every day for at least 28 days (a lunar cycle) to shift old patterns and help integrate new behaviours. Listening to Michael discourse on specific aspects of the spiritual path, I could feel myself reviewing each aspect in my life and seeing where I gave into fear, or got defensive, or bought into other people's egoic opinions, or tried to process their realities. Hearing Michael discourse on all aspects of life, philosophy, metaphysics, alchemy and ethics is one of the great joys in life. To experience him distill profound spiritual truths into easily accessible, digestible, and actionable realties is to experience true alchemy in a very grounded manner. He talks on such a wide variety of topics: from the very down to earth aspects of our day-to-day existence, to far out philosophical and universal concepts. Each session is like being taken on a trip through the Cosmos and back again.

Michael energetically overlights the CDs, specifically tailoring them to each individual's unique energy frequency, and we get to work with an incredible amount of support from higher energies. Every time I sit down and listen to a CD, I get taken on this immense inner journey that helps me to wake up to self-defeating patterns and to bring more love to my experience, so that I can heal those tendencies and choose a more loving and wise choice.

To give you some kind of cup to put it in, it is quite similar (but energetically much deeper) to when you listen to an amazing piece of music or watch a moving film and suddenly the solidity of the external world dissolves all around you and you are swept into a deep inner journey full of insight and revelation. Picture that, but while experiencing a spiritual discourse from Michael that is energetically tailored to you and supported to activate awakening in you. What Michael facilitates is true magic, through and through. There's no better word to describe it!

Even though I was living on the opposite side of Australia from him, as I engaged in all of these courses and CDs, the learning always felt so energetically alive, tailored, and juicy; like he was right next to me, walking beside me, every step of the way.

This is another one of those experiences that sound made up, but I assure that this is all very real. Until you've actually gone through and experienced it for yourself, it will sound far-fetched.

As I write this, I realise that this is one of the major threads that weave through all that I share about what it's like learning from Michael and all that he offers: that magic is a tangible force, present in every atom and moment of life, and the all-encompassing nature of divine love is both all around us and within us.

I share this with you to give you a glimpse of what is possible in life. To crack open another reality within you, for you to **know** deep within you that when you commit to this path with sincerity, and seek the wisdom of an exemplary guide, you can unlock life's mysteries, grow from them, and align your life to serve this higher calling and the greater good. It doesn't get better than that! Trust me, I've tried the other dead-end lanes.

Because I was living over East and the Cosmosis® Mentoring Centre was based in Perth, I didn't get a lot of time to be in the same room as Michael, but once or twice a year I would go over for a retreat, which would be an incredibly accelerated time of growth, dissolving the old fears and moving into more expansion of the new.

The retreats are an opportunity to disconnect from our day-to-day lives (all the challenges and stresses of that) and to be cocooned in high spiritual energies and frequencies, in order to facilitate accelerated change and growth within us. Students from all over the country and all over the world come to work on themselves; to heal, grow, and learn from Michael.

The retreats are some of the most incredible experiences I've ever had in this life. They are a mixture of deep emotional, psychological and spiritual investigation into what makes us tick, while experiencing a kind of utopian way of living and, at the same time, being supported to face and transform all kinds of self-created hells within ourselves, all rolled into one. They are full of expansion and transformation, but also deeply confronting.

One of the big things that I have learnt over my time working with Michael is to develop my ability to confront my own bullshit and resistances. To face my own fears, doubts, and disbeliefs head on is not an easy thing to do. But like any skill, it is a muscle that can be trained, and the stronger we develop it, the more we're able to work *with* Life and not *fight* her every step of the way.

I feel to share some of the earlier experiences of working with Michael during those retreats, because in some ways they were the hardest and most confusing for a fledgling initiate. As I've developed more courage, and am less in my own way, the work has become somewhat smoother and more graceful lately - still always tremendously confronting and challenging, but definitely more mature.

Early on when working with him, even though he was constantly championing me, I was so battered and bruised inside that if he ever reflected some part of my own entitlement back at me, or helped me to see how much I was trying to make up for my deep unworthiness and sense of failure (by puffing myself up, or trying be special), then I would take that very personally and be really rocked by it. It's important to note the difference between someone championing you as a soul, compared to affirming your negative ego (or, in other words, enabling your dysfunctional behaviour). Constant acceptance of those negative ego patterns isn't helping anybody and so, oftentimes, the most efficient way to champion soul evolution is by confronting the negative ego, however uncomfortable that may be.

Michael was always trying to help me through that, but early on I took a lot of stuff personally and I was looking through a wounded lens. My notions of love were all twisted and screwy. I'd never really experienced someone lovingly and directly calling me on my bullshit at the same time. To palpably feel both of those qualities simultaneously is incredibly healing, but initially it was very confusing. So many people in the world only have one part of the equation - they may be very loving and encouraging but also overly indulgent and permissive, or they may be strict disciplinarians but lack any deep kindness or love. This is one overarching aspect that Michael helps all his students with; supporting them to disentangle all of the faulty beliefs about love they've picked up along the way. He is like a very clear, stark mirror or a resonant tuning fork, emanating deep psychological clarity and heart purity, and assisting us to shed all that is disharmonious within us.

'You've got to stop looking for love and worth outside of you. That's an inside job.'

I had so much confusion with my self-esteem. I felt deep levels of unworthiness but also felt quite skilled in certain areas. I was trying to overcome all the weaknesses by forcing myself into positivity and confidence. But in reality, I was just rejecting the wounded parts within me and overcompensating by adding more layers of pride, self-righteousness, and entitlement. As the days went by, he helped me to see how much I took things personally, and made it mean all these things about me. I was so caught up in trying to please people and keep the peace, but it was such a dysfunctional pattern that kept me looping in self-defeating habits; desperately trying to fit in, but selling myself, and my authenticity, out as a result.

'As long as you keep taking things personally, you're just maintaining, protecting, and preserving your egoic identity. That's not who you are. It'll keep you in separation from the Oneness of all life, at odds with the Universe. And if you keep making meaning (building all those imagined narratives) out of every little thing that happens, then you'll just keep yourself stuck. It's just life happening. Feel as you feel without judgment. Those feelings coming up to be healed are not happening now. Let go of the past and transform your reality.'

In those early days, I was quite uncoachable. I was coming out of a place where, previously, my teachers and guardians were so clumsy, critical, or absent in their approach to me, that I developed a strong self-reliance, and was fiercely protective of that. At the time, this approach served me, as it was a way to keep the dysfunction out as I tried to steer my life to something more stable and steady.

The process of starting to trust people to guide me again took a little while, and it was a little bumpy.

I can only imagine how tedious it must have been for Michael to endure my endless testing, as I tiptoed around some of his ideas, weighing them carefully and examining them thoroughly from all angles, cautious and hesitant in my progress. My journey was often a dance of four steps forward, then three steps back (not the most effective way to grow long-term). A lot of those patterns were coming out of my fear of making big mistakes and going off track (like I'd done in the past), but eventually those fears had to be transcended too.

He was always so loving and patient, never rushing me or forcing me to "get" something. He was also strong and direct when he needed to be, helping me to get my head out of my arse in moments, which was very useful to help crack through some of my control and stubbornness.

Michael is endlessly resourceful in guiding his student's growth, always grounded in the highest ethics and with a wonderfully spirited and disarming sense of humour. His honesty is so refreshing - often very direct, unadorned, and raw. But he is never harming with the truth, for that wouldn't be helpful to anyone. In a world drenched in pretence, falsehoods, and empty flattery, to be around someone that tells it like it is, is such a refreshing and needed realignment and reorientation that is sorely lacking today.

However, in those early days, working closely with someone who I admired so deeply was really confronting. Michael's greatness has always been, and remains, a source of profound inspiration, yet his very presence often starkly mirrored back to me how much I'd fallen short of courage in my own journey, in past lives. To feel him championing my potential in every moment, whilst also nudging me to confront the foolish choices of past lives (healing old wounds and fears), was no easy journey – it demanded humility and a depth of maturity. It brings to mind the brilliant quote form Carl Jung - "People will do anything, no matter how absurd, in order to avoid facing their own soul."

Michael gently asks me, 'Can you let go of seeing it as failure? Have you learnt something from it? Every moment is an opportunity to learn, grow, and become a little wiser; to evolve. The more you take things personally, the more humiliated you will be by the experience. If you keep judging it, then you'll keep playing out that dysfunctional pattern. But if you don't take it personally, and allow the feeling to move through you, then you can work with it in a mature way. You'll be able to transform the feeling and truly let go of the past. It will be more of a humbling experience for you. Can you feel the subtle difference in that?'

I could definitely feel into the truth of what he was sharing, but I found it difficult to grapple with because of the judgement I had for the foolish choices which had been previously made. I could feel into the brighter aspects of my soul, but the baggage that was also in there had left its marks, and I still struggled with that. My soul felt like a once pristine, crisp-white canvas which had now become a crumpled, desecrated mess - all twisted, creased, and bent out of shape. The process of undoing that mess, smoothing out the marks and creases, would be necessary. However, underneath each creased and crumpled part was some wounding and some defensive part trying to protect the pain within me. It would take confront and courage to be able to acknowledge the choices I had made to get to this point – to take full responsibility for creating my life in this way – and from there it would be possible to undo some of those choices and to open up to a new path and destiny.

This leads me to ask an essential question for all seekers: do we truly want to actualise greatness, or do we just like the idea of it? Do we have the courage and the self-determination to bring that spark to life within us, or do we settle for admiring greatness from afar? Deep down, are we content with our familiar, miserable mediocrity? Would we prefer to stay in that, make excuses, blame, and find a way to stay in victimhood? Or do we want to be rattled out of our comfort zones, and see how deep the rabbit hole can go?

Some of my most profound lessons have taken months, sometimes years, to truly settle within me. But in retrospect they have often been the most empowering insights long-term.

In the early days, Michael would, at times, reflect something back for me that I wasn't able to fully understand and appreciate till months or years later. In the early days, there was some scepticism as I debated whether to let go of deep core beliefs that I had lived out of for several years, previously believing them to be true. But as I worked through them, saw the illusions and lies that I'd bought into, and felt the freedom on the other side of that, my life would change, and this was incredibly empowering.

Building up the confront to let go of deeper and longer held dysfunctional patterns is a major aspect of the work. Initially it feels like the sky is going to come crashing down and the world is going to end, and then when it doesn't, and your life gets more amazing, expansive, and empowered, then it becomes very exciting.

Over a couple of years, as I moved through those initial fears and terrors and let go of self-imposed conditions and limitations, the next layers of possibility opened up. My experience of the energetic cocooning in the retreats deepened, and the constant, intense, unconditional love that Michael held me in became more profound in its healing. So many of the blocked and broken parts within me started to melt.

Reaching this stage, I started to have more prolonged experiences of oneness. It was no longer something that I only experienced in meditation. Now I was able to actually walk around and interact with people during retreat and continue to experience oneness. This was a key milestone in my growth. I started to get glimpses of all of life being a moving meditation.

As Michael and the Energies supported me to practice that during retreat, it gave me hope that I could possibly learn how to do that in the wider world while not on retreat, and maybe even one day hold that state of being in my own right (without the training wheels on). Feeling so many of my self-imposed conditions and limitations dissolve helps me to see just how illusory they really are, and this gives me a lot of hope to move through the next layers of my negative ego, to ground more of the Spirit that I AM. This is incredibly empowering, and I start to understand that these long-held beliefs and experiences aren't really "Who I Am". I can let go of them. And if I can let go of them, then what else can I let go of?

As I healed the old wounds and cleared beliefs that'd been stuck for several years, I found the courage to clear deeper wounds and patterns I'd carried for a decade. Healing the layers of that decade gave me the strength to confront and release even more entrenched beliefs from childhood. From there, I felt brave enough to face beliefs and wounds that had shaped me over recent lifetimes, which showed me that it was possible to clear old, buried traumas from ancient lives throughout history. I started to sense how deep the rabbit hole could go and realised that so many of the beliefs of "Who I Am" are simply old experiences of limitation. They're just costumes that need to be shed to access a deeper truth of my Source Self.

Once I started to get some momentum with clearing those old wounds and beliefs, then the growth accelerated in many areas of my life. In other words, I took the brakes off. What a relief!

Overtime, life has become very, very interesting; a great adventure and quest! Some might say I'm on a "Hero's Journey". I'm still very much a work in progress but I'm truly loving this journey of self-discovery. Michael continually holds the bar high (a sign of deep respect), and constantly gives me access to the next layer that I feel inspired and compelled to work with. But the difference now is that instead of feeling my own failure and falling in a heap, I see it as a huge gift that I can actually do something about; I can transform my life and offer some of that hope to my community and the world at large. He has helped me to be truly grateful, not just for the breakthroughs, but for all of the challenges. That is a huge gift! Thank you, thank you, thank you!

Before I bring my story to an end, there is a final observation I'd like to offer.

It is one thing to learn a specific craft from a skilled teacher and become more proficient in that particular skill. But it's another thing entirely to be guided by a true spiritual teacher, for the spiritual teacher doesn't teach you just one particular skill. What they share with you is how to heal all of the blocks that you've put in place which prevent you from allowing Divine Love to flow through you, and how to live a purposeful and meaningful life serving the Evolutionary Forces. That learning ripples though all areas of the student's life.

Michael has profoundly cracked open my life and helped me to reawaken my soul and the possibilities for a life well-lived. He has not only opened up my acting craft in immeasurable ways, he has also set the entire spectrum of my life force ablaze with a newfound vitality. Coming from a place of feeling so shut down and blocked inside of myself, his influence on me has been profound, to say the least.

However, I am not special. His presence and his influence does that for all of his students, uniquely. Here are a few of the varied areas of life and professions he has worked with and affected; doctors and nurses, counsellors and psychologists, coaches and mentors, healers and naturopaths, teachers and artists - to name but a few. All of them have been profoundly inspired by his influence and are living more purposeful and selfless lives as a result. In turn, they have all affected significant change in their communities and fields of endeavour.

This is not an exercise in lionising or mythologising a man that I have deep love and respect for. It is a process of attempting to accurately convey the very real, nuts-and-bolts experience of what he embodies and also what he has so generously offered to me and all of his students. My hope is that it will give you an opportunity to sense what could be possible for you and others, and how that could ignite a flame within you and create a monumental groundswell through all of our communities and networks. This is a glimpse of what is actually possible if people believe in the power of alchemical transformation, and are willing to put the work in.

There are countless more stories to share about all the ways he has raised people up, but in essence what Michael has done so successfully through founding the Comsosis® Mentoring Centre is that he has created a home for spiritual seekers and initiates from all walks of life, who have travelled many varied paths. He has offered us all a place to heal our soul baggage, and accelerate our potential individually and collectively, beyond anything we believed was possible. We have been gifted an opportunity to work closely with like-minded and like-hearted souls - united in purpose; all striving to bring a brighter future to humanity.

To get to experience even a fraction of that sacredness and deep ethical integrity feels incredibly hopeful in a world that is often so riddled with corruption and degradation. Part of the reason why many groups, in all areas of life, haven't been able to succeed is because of all that corruption and degradation. All the internal politics and ego games get in the way of group harmony and then hinder group success and collective achievement. But if that's able to be cleared (as I have hopefully illustrated in this chapter), then people can band together and be forces for change, evolution, and greater good in the world. We are stronger together and, together, we become exponentially greater than the sum of our parts!

STORY SEVEN

~ ~ ~

What's That Got to do With Grounding and Expressing Love?

It wasn't until I met Michael that I began to understand why life wasn't straightforward and why life was equally so serendipitous and surprising.

In 2003, Michael had arranged a festive gathering near Melbourne where, in his inimitable and generous way, he had invited colleagues and like-minded metaphysicians, musicians, light-workers and seekers from around the globe to come together for several days of presentation, music, and workshops. A metaphysician-healer, who'd help me shift DNA after an extreme prognosis, suggested that I'd find it useful. And it was. It was also refreshing, instructive, hopeful, uplifting and fulfilled a longing for connectivity.

During Michael's discourses, the endless peace that infused the large auditorium of attendees and countless unseens was palpable. His humour and theatrics were confronting yet compelling. As he readily stated, 'This is for the entertainment of your egos; the real work is happening at soul level'.

I clocked that he was an old friend, but I was too self-conscious and confused to act on it decisively. It was also dawning on me just how much I continued to evade being here on planet Earth, even though my love for Her was boundless.

It was evident that Michael was using music to assist us in energetic clearing processes to unravel our fears and our judgments. Bundled in whatever version of trauma, avoidance, denial or pain, those fear-based experiences manifested to be cleared in order to awaken latent or new psychological clarity. It was a seamless experience which everyone experienced uniquely, in their individual feeling and understanding, which we excitedly shared over meals. It still feels far-out, clear and true.

Musically, twenty years on, he's learnt guitar and fronts The Love Finders Band, still doing sonic resonating which is out there to enjoy.

In 2004, Michael invited a troop of aspirants, mostly from Australia, America, the UK and the Continent, where my partner and I were living at the time, to tour some of the great sacred sites of southern England. It began with a spiritual conference with workshops and continued as a practical experiential university of opening awareness. After one of the lectures, Michael gave me a friendly hug and an unexpected electrical blast, from his heart to mine, that would have catapulted me across the room if I wasn't in an embrace, awoke me from whatever malaise I was permanently in.

After that, on tour, I couldn't stop looking at him and I felt quite awkward and rude about it, knowing that there was much past and future learning, growth and understanding that I could gain from him. I knew that he could teach me what a life well-lived in the present could be.

Michael shared insight into the heightened energies at sacred sites of stone circles, crop circles and cathedrals, both ruined and operational with their centuries of artisanship. We learnt of the significance of the Arthurian enactment, ideals and mysteries, as examples of the contributing bedrock of balanced political functionality. We learnt of how the Romans brought their flavour of social sophistication and we visited like-minded initiates.

But it was the forests of ancient lived wisdom, with their 1000-year-old oak, that drove home a collective living depositary of consecutive time. It remains an indelible experience that birthed new respect for time's opportunities and spatialisation, and which gifted me an experience of truth and connectivity across timelines. As experiences go, this was far-out!

Since then, an incremental unfurling awareness has been part and parcel of my daily experience. And Michael has been there the whole time, steady, guiding, cajoling and confronting when necessary, sharing the vastness of his experience, encouraging, reflecting bullshit, yet remaining completely unmoved and patient with the chaos we individuals may outplay. He is tenacious, precocious, careful, tender, direct yet gentle, very funny and serious. He has high and enduring ethics, he is respectful, fiercely loving, kind, compassionate, and he does not enable selfishness, stupidity or laziness.

He encourages us in all regards to address and explore our character, our inner landscape, our exaggerations and our frailty across all bandwidths. Most of us humans respond and react to our livings via the lens of our dysfunction. As we accept ourselves and do away with the distorting lenses, the inner ruckus quietens. This makes for a wholeness of character rather than a fractured and idiosyncratic persona. This experience of wholeness connects the individual with "all that they are", which is a very rich largess indeed, far greater and much more expansive than the three-dimensional human presentation.

Through the Cosmosis® Mentoring Centre, I've learnt that we have our own maps and signposts that allow us to unravel ourselves, release tied up energy and establish more wholeness and equanimity. It's shown to us, step by step, how to navigate this tender psychological landscape, with its unique formatting, as we return to untrammelled integrity and balance.

At the end of the written and audio material you'll see or hear the phrase, 'May Love Restore the Balance'. This is neither sentimental nor fluffy, it's a statement of achievable self-restoration.

After these initial meetings with Michael, it took a few more years before I joined the Cosmosis® Mentoring Centre as a mentee and a student. When I did, it was a "coming home" experience.

It became apparent that much of our early patterning and programming remains with us unless we actively choose to address and maturate those aspects of ourselves. Setting sail on one's own discovery channel is a very rewarding, sometimes frustrating and confronting, but thoroughly worthwhile process. The victim identifications, the "not fair"s, the judgemental parts, the taking things personally, the doubts and fears, once recognised and addressed, fall by the wayside as they are superseded by profound acceptance and a recognition that you are part of a much larger self. A leaf on a tree, so to speak. As Michael shares, 'It's simple, but it's not necessarily easy'. If you apply the tools, however, you'll prevail.

My go-to escape, while growing up, was a fluid obsession with fine arts. Art became something that I could explore and hide behind, an oasis against the backdrop of being unable to fully "get" numeracy and literacy, which baffled those around me, causing them frustration. Feeling as though I simply couldn't keep up with the expectation, I threw esteem out the window and the arts became a sanctuary.

Back then, education was often reactive and dyslexia, in its various forms, was largely unidentified. In the familial space, I could feel parental anxiety. This caused me to feel as though there was something fundamentally wrong with me and yet, at the same time, I could understand their concern. So, I ended up faking a lot as a kid, using personality as a trick and a decoy to reduce all those dynamics. Art, music and natural history were wildly intoxicating and appreciated topics at home and so, in that environment, I felt safe. At school, however, I did not.

Though I loved music, I let it go at the age of 15 because, in my dyslexic state, I couldn't read the leger-lines of dancing notes which seemed to be moving about on the page, doing their own thing. I also preferred to use the practise time to paint. Self-consciousness often sucked up sensitivities.

Art School was the place to be and there, I began meditating – it was, after all, the early 70's and we were all up for it. In retrospect, the meditation that I was doing was probably the best thing available at the time, but by the end of the 1990's, while living in the UK, I irrevocably stopped meditating on the day that Princess Diana died – suddenly, I just couldn't do "connection" in that manner anymore. It triggered a chasm. After 24 years as a consistent and passionate meditator, following a karma yoga path, my devotion had vanished. I'd lived in India, I'd studied Ayurveda in depth across the various disciplines, and I was engaged in interesting projects. But one day, I simply lost interest. Baffled, I couldn't explain myself to friends or even family.

Sure, I learnt a lot about spatialisation from all those years of bliss, but elevating out of the body into transcendence (what I called "loping across the universe") suddenly seemed out of place.

Over time, it became apparent that "not being here now" compromises your "house". If you keep leaving it unguarded, the stress that the body undergoes when you switch to automatic pilot can be quite debilitating for the bodies.

When you are not present, you are not acting as the captain of your own ship and, in your absence, the ego takes over that role. The ego's natural role is to keep the body alive. If you leave the ego in control, it naturally begins to respond to life as though everything is a threat. It goes into overwhelm, attempting to keep itself and the body safe from its reactive and defensive standpoint. The ego cannot perceive of the soul's reality – its viewpoint is limited and reactive.

The soul has a much vaster vista, seeing far ahead and understanding the significance of life's experiences. Rather than being reactive, the soul is deliberate and responsive, able to dance with life, understanding the intent and the purpose behind phenomena. Unlike the ego, the soul is an apt captain of the ship – it is calm, considered, present, and able to intelligently respond to life and its challenges.

The ego is best soothed when it is under the care and guidance of the soul. When we "step out" of the body, we rob the ego of proper parenting and its most stabilising influence, and then the ego acts out, desperately, as it attempts to protect itself and its body from perceived (but unreal) threats.

By blissing out and having our reality in higher planes of existence, quite cut off from the reality of the form world, we demand that the ego do a job that it doesn't have the software for. Then, when we step back in to the body, we look around us at the mess which has been made, and we glimpse the terrified monster that our egos have become, and we blame the ego – we blame the human part of us, and then we recoil in judgement and, instead of staying, cleaning up the mess, taking responsibility, and providing proper parenting, we step out once more.

How self-righteous and how neglectful, to abandon life here in order to experience love and light, all while causing damage and harm to the very part of us which most requires this love and light, and blaming the part of us which we abandoned for everything which is not love and light… It was quite humbling and quietening to see how much of a zealot and just how un-spiritual I'd actually been.

Back on the sacred site tour in 2004, I had mumbled something to Michael about my previous experiences with meditation, and about the abrupt ending of this phase of my life. Understanding that I was totally ignorant to my lack of presence, and knowing that, at that stage, I was clueless about the survival habits that I'd cultivated in my absence, Michael asked, 'What's that got to do with grounding and expressing love? How is floating around upstairs going to help bring the love here?' My response was that I didn't know.

He explained that it's pointless building light-bodies if you don't ground the love and the light that you cultivate to move through you, bringing them into these realms where they can be of most benefit. If it's not actualised, then it amounts to nothing – anything which is attained outside of the body will simply evaporate at the end of the incarnation. The soul learns through felt and lived experience.

The soul already exists in those higher dimensional states – it remains unaltered if you spend your whole life floating around in its reality. The soul puts forth a body so that it can learn about bringing its reality here – so that it can have the felt and lived experience of translating higher energy into visceral, tangible and service-oriented phenomena. The soul only undergoes evolution – is only changed – if you be fully here, present in the body, finding and exploring new ways to ground and express love. A life spent loping across the universe is, in evolutionary terms, rather a wasted one.

Michael spoke of ascending-descension, his description of the evolution of the soul (ascension) through the ongoing grounding (descension) of one's greater self. This process involves making space for those higher energies to move through you, as conduit, into the planetary systems and realms.

That was the beginning of a whole new reimagining of what was possible if you were actually present in a body. From there, it took years to learn how to "stay", and to this day it remains something that I attend to.

Amongst that band of travelling tourists were woven histories, soul-remembrances, reflections of the past, Michael's discourses, and process journeys. We learnt tools for running energetic clearing processes whilst visiting sites that generated more of the same.

In every sense, Michael has changed, as you'd expect from someone on an accelerated journey. But he hasn't left anyone or anywhere to do so – he's continued doing and bringing the same work of assisting those 'who have the eyes see, the ears to hear and the heart to recognise' to follow their knowing, grounding and expressing love through their own unique contribution.

Over the next decades, the innate organic desire to grow increased significantly – it's expansive. The irrepressible enthusiasm for life and curiosity I had as a kid remains, though it is a lot more balanced and discerning. I really enjoy being here in this life and participating in the livings, not trying to get out of myself, or to be lofty, but just being okay with where life is at. In many ways, Michael has encouraged me back here from never-never land, for which I'm immensely grateful.

Michael has the knack, as initiates do, of being able to present the same themes in a myriad of ways so as touch as many different souls, over and over again, at whatever stage of their evolutionary journey they are at, and no matter how present (or not) they are in that moment. His teachings are layered with knowing.

The breadth of coverage is a veritable Ancient Alexandrian library of knowledge which is offered through discourses, musings and applicable processes that the individual can use as tools to access the occult and mystical gnosis within, bringing vision, virtue and value to all.

STORY EIGHT

~~~

Introduction: The Recognition

I remember the moment vividly, as though it had just happened. It was late, and I had just finished saying goodnight to the kids. As I came down the stairs, passing the sitting room, something stopped me in my tracks. A video was playing on the TV, and though I can't recall the exact words or topic, it wasn't what was being said that drew me in. It was the energy behind it – the feeling that drew me in like a tractor beam.

In that instant, there was a moment of profound recognition. I didn't know Michael personally at that point, yet it felt as though I did. It wasn't just familiarity – it was deeper, like stumbling upon an old friend from a time beyond this lifetime. That energetic pull, that recognition, was unmistakable. Something within me shifted, and I knew I had to learn more.

That moment marked the beginning of my journey with Michael – a journey that would lead to immense growth, moments of joy, and deep, sometimes uncomfortable introspection. But none of that was in my mind at the time. All I knew was that I had found an energy which resonated with me in a way that was both entirely new and deeply familiar.

Looking back, I can see that this connection wasn't initially about his words or teachings. It was about Michael's presence. Even from the briefest glimpse on the screen, I could feel something beyond the surface. I wouldn't have called it a spiritual recognition back then; I had little experience with spiritual teachers or groups. But despite my unfamiliarity with that world, I knew there was something about Michael that I needed to explore more deeply.

Shortly after that night, I found myself embarking on the mentoring journey that would come to shape the years that followed. At first, I had no expectations – I wasn't sure what I was stepping into. But the connection was undeniable. It didn't take long before Michael's influence began to weave itself into my life, subtly at first, and then with increasing clarity and intensity.

Our first real meeting mirrored that initial recognition on the screen. There was no grand entrance, no "guru" presence as some might expect from a spiritual teacher. He was grounded, real. We spoke of motorcycles, cars, and engineering – passions he held with a genuine curiosity and intensity. That was part of what drew me in further – his groundedness. Here was someone who would eventually guide me into the depths of spiritual evolution, yet he was approachable, human, and profoundly relatable.

What I didn't realise then was that this seemingly chance moment wasn't just an isolated event. It was the beginning of a journey that would challenge me, stretch my understanding of who I was, and uncover parts of myself I hadn't known were there. It was the start of an accelerated path of transformation, a journey that would become a cornerstone of my life for the coming decades.

What continues to strike me, even today, is Michael's constancy. From that first recognition to now, he has remained unwavering – an anchor of self-mastery and wisdom. Whether I am lost, resistant, or struggling, Michael remains steady. His consistency, his ability to maintain his self-mastery no matter what life has brought him, has been both inspiring and confronting. I've never met anyone who embodies such a steady, enduring presence. Whether in moments of joy or difficulty, whether I was moving forward or retreating in my personal evolution, Michael is always there. More than often, he gently reminds me of who I truly am and the direction we are heading in.

It was a simple moment that set all of this in motion – a video on a screen. Yet, from that one moment, I knew this life would never quite be the same. What started as a fleeting encounter has since become one of the most significant and transformative relationships of my life. For that recognition, I remain deeply grateful every day.

Early Mentoring Experiences: Indirect Guidance and Personal Growth

My early mentoring experiences with Michael were unlike anything I had encountered before. Without prescribing actions or offering explicit instructions, he would guide me subtly, encouraging self-reflection and self-discovery rather than providing direct answers. His presence prompted me to look within, fostering introspection that led to deeper self-awareness. Over time, I came to value the power of discovering my own truths through his indirect guidance.

At first, this approach felt disorienting. I had anticipated a clear path laid out before me, but instead, I was met with gentle questions and suggestions that resonated only after I had time to reflect. One of my earliest insights came during our first retreat together. Before the event, Michael requested a specific World War II artefact – a peculiar ask, considering we had only recently met. I didn't question it at the time, but in hindsight, I see it as an early sign of Michael's ability to recognise aspects of me that I hadn't yet seen in myself. His request wasn't about the artefact itself; it was an invitation to connect and build trust, marking the beginning of a mentoring journey that would continually push me toward self-discovery.

Through these experiences, I learned that Michael's gift wasn't in giving answers but in helping me ask the right questions. His mentoring was never about dictating what I should do, but rather about showing me the choices in front of me. He held up a mirror to my life, allowing me to see my patterns and behaviours with newfound clarity. This empowered me to take responsibility for my journey, to make decisions from a place of understanding.

As time passed, I realised that Michael's approach was exactly what I needed. He knew when to step back and when to challenge me, often sensing the bigger picture when I was lost in the details. In moments when I felt stuck or overwhelmed, he wouldn't provide solutions but would offer just enough insight to help me find my way through. While this was sometimes frustrating, it led to more meaningful growth and lasting change.

This pattern repeated over the years. Whenever I encountered what felt like a wall, Michael would present an idea which initially seemed vague, but which later unfolded into a profound realisation. By encouraging me to own my journey fully, he allowed me to experience growth through my own efforts, making each lesson deeply personal and transformative. Looking back, I see that Michael's subtle guidance created the space for me to discover, evolve, and ultimately trust in my own path.

The Band: Growth Through Challenge

One of the most unexpected and transformative experiences I've had with Michael is being a member of The Love Finders Band. When the idea of forming a band first came up, it felt distant, almost like a side project. But as I came to understand, there was never anything casual in Michael's approach – every interaction carries purpose. What began as a simple jam session quickly became a profound journey that pushed me beyond what I thought I was capable of, both musically and spiritually.

From the first session, it was clear that Michael had a vision. He wasn't content with us just "playing around". True to his nature, he saw something much bigger for us and knew how to guide us there. His leadership took us from a loose group of budding musicians into a cohesive band. It was Michael who ensured we weren't just learning songs but stepping into something more expansive with each rehearsal, each performance. He pushed us beyond our comfort zones – not just musically but in a full life experience.

Michael's approach to rehearsals was never about perfection or technical mastery alone. He understands that real growth comes from much more than learning your part on an instrument. When we rehearsed, he wasn't just interested in whether we could play our parts correctly; he wanted us to play as a band, to feel the energy between us and let that guide the music. He knew the deeper work wasn't about the notes but about confronting the limitations within ourselves and within our interactions.

In those early days, I wasn't an experienced musician, and the challenges were significant. But Michael's constant challenge – done with both love and firmness – revealed parallels between the band and my spiritual journey. Just as in the band, spiritual growth required discipline, practice, and a willingness to face discomfort for the sake of something greater. Michael's presence in the band was always about more than the music; it was about transformation.

One of the most challenging moments came on the day of our first event, when a band member – someone I had been particularly close to – was tragically killed in a car accident. Michael became an example of how to feel fully while also holding steady. His ability to grieve without collapsing into the grief, to honour the loss while still guiding us forward, was a profound lesson. It was through his leadership that we eventually returned to the band room, found our footing again, and moved forward, carrying the deeper understanding that Michael had helped us realise.

Michael's ability to challenge us was one of the most remarkable aspects of the band experience. He never let us stay comfortable. Whether it was learning more complex songs, incorporating new styles, or stepping onto bigger stages, he constantly expanded our horizons. But it wasn't just about the music – it was about the energy we brought, the connection we fostered as a group, and the sense of service in every performance. Michael taught us that the purpose of the band wasn't just to play songs; it was to offer something beyond ourselves, to create a space of love and connection and joy, both within the band and with our audience.

Teamwork was another major lesson I took from the band, one that Michael facilitated. While I had experienced teamwork before in sports and the workplace, it wasn't until the band that I truly understood the depth of connection that comes from working as one unit. Michael showed us how to adapt in real time, how to support each other in ways that went beyond the music. There were moments on stage where things didn't go as planned, but Michael's influence had taught us to cover for each other, to read the energy of the group, and to keep the performance flowing.

Through the band, Michael also pushed me to confront deeper emotional patterns that I had carried for years. As a drummer, the physical discomfort I experienced during rehearsals and performances – tight shoulders, sore arms, sore muscles – wasn't just physical. Michael helped me see that the discomfort stemmed from emotional barriers that were being brought to the surface through the intensity of our work together. His presence created an environment where I could begin to release these emotional blocks, freeing me to experience not only more ease in my body, but more depth in my music and in my life.

One of the most profound moments in this journey came when Michael had a custom drum riser built for me. At the time, I was dealing with a serious back issue that made it difficult to perform. Initially, I saw the riser as an imposition – a heavy addition to my already challenging set up. But Michael, ever aware, pointed out my lack of gratitude. That simple observation shifted something fundamental within me. It wasn't just about the riser; it was about recognising that my state didn't have to be dictated by my physical condition. Gratitude was a choice I could make, regardless of what I was feeling. That experience helped me see how I could curtail serving based on how I felt. Hardly unconditional.

In another moment of deep insight, Michael once referred to my "demeanour of disapproval" during a band session. It was a simple sentence, but it hit like a bomb. What struck me most about this sharing was how it just felt so spot on. I could not have put it so succinctly, accurately or with greater impact. His words captured something I hadn't fully acknowledged in myself – a tendency to judge and energetically disapprove of others. It was another instance of Michael's ability to reflect back the truth, even when it was uncomfortable. But like every other instance, it was also an invitation to grow beyond that pattern. That one sentence has unlocked incredible insight into so much of me that lived in the unconscious. Bringing that into my conscious awareness has provided a rich vein of character development that I continue to work with every day.

Looking back, the band is one of the most challenging and rewarding parts of my journey with Michael. It isn't just about learning to play music; it is about letting go – trust in myself, allow the process, and have confidence in the people around me. Michael's leadership continually pushes us to expand, to step into our mastery even when we don't feel ready.

Through the band, I continue to learn that growth comes through challenge. It's not easy, and it's rarely comfortable, but it's in those moments of discomfort that we truly begin to evolve. Michael created the space for me to confront my self-imposed limitations, to seriously work with them and, in doing so, to connect more deeply with myself, with those around me, and with the love that underlies everything we do.

Masculinity: A Journey of Confrontation and Acceptance

One of the most challenging aspects of my journey with Michael has been confronting my understanding of masculinity. Before working with him, I hadn't fully realised how much judgement I carried around being a man. I felt disconnected from traditional expressions of masculinity, often seeing them as rooted in aggression, dominance, or emotional repression. In distancing myself from these traits, I ended up rejecting a significant part of myself, leaning into what I perceived to be more feminine qualities as a way of coping, rather than achieving true balance.

Michael presented a different model of masculinity – grounded, steady, and deeply accepting. He embodied a form of strength that was firm yet compassionate, assertive yet open. His example challenged my own judgements and gradually revealed where I had been holding back from embracing my own masculine energy. It wasn't immediate; his presence and expression of balanced masculinity held up a mirror to my own discomfort and resistance, forcing me to confront my biases and unresolved beliefs over time.

What struck me most about Michael was his seamless integration of masculine and feminine energies. He didn't reject one for the other but instead allowed both to coexist harmoniously. Through his example, I began to see that masculinity wasn't inherently flawed or "toxic" – it was how I had been taught to express it that needed refining. Michael's influence showed me that healthy masculinity is rooted in love, integrity, and presence, not control or dominance.

This realisation allowed me to reframe my relationship with masculinity. I saw that my discomfort wasn't about masculinity itself but about unacknowledged patterns and societal conditioning that I had internalised. Michael's ability to embody strength and tenderness in equal measure showed me that it was possible to be both strong and sensitive, assertive and compassionate. Over time, I began to integrate these aspects, letting go of my judgements and embracing a more balanced expression of myself.

Even now, this is an ongoing journey. While old patterns sometimes resurface, I now have the tools to confront and transform them. Michael has shown me that true mastery is not about perfection but about the willingness to continually refine and accept oneself fully.

In a world where masculinity is often scrutinised, I've come to see that the path forward isn't about rejecting the masculine, but about embracing it with love and balance. For that, I am deeply grateful to Michael, who has shown me that it's possible to be both grounded and expansive, both masculine and feminine.

Self-Mastery and Mentoring: The Journey of Consistent Growth

Throughout my journey with Michael, his unwavering self-mastery has been a constant source of inspiration – and, at times, confrontation. I have been repeatedly struck by his ability to remain steady and aligned, regardless of external circumstances. This consistency has challenged me to examine my own patterns and areas where I fall short, revealing just how much room I have left to grow. Michael embodies self-mastery in a way that is less about perfection and more about remaining grounded in love and awareness, no matter what arises.

One example of this mentoring happened not long after I arrived in Perth. We were working on a construction project in his garage, casually discussing various topics, including Telstra, my employer at the time. Like many Australians, I had plenty of frustrations to share about Telstra. After listening for a while, Michael quietly observed, 'We've spent the last few minutes doing nothing but complaining about Telstra.' His words stopped me in my tracks, making me realise how automatic – and unconscious – my complaining had become. The moment wasn't about Telstra; it was about becoming more deliberate with my attention and energy, especially in my relationships. Michael didn't judge or correct me; he simply invited me to reflect. That subtle, shared insight prompted me to become more conscious and intentional in my communication.

This interaction captures the essence of Michael's mentoring. Rather than giving answers, he creates opportunities for self-reflection, allowing me to find my own way. He encourages self-mastery by holding up a mirror, showing me my patterns and behaviours without imposing his will. There were times when I wanted direct guidance, especially when I felt lost or unsure, but Michael would instead give me just enough insight to find my own path forward. This process, while sometimes uncomfortable, has ultimately allowed me to grow more deeply and independently.

Michael's consistency has also been a mirror, constantly highlighting areas where I am not yet aligned. Being around someone who holds such a high level of self-mastery can be challenging because it reveals your own limitations. There have been moments when I felt inadequate or doubtful in his presence, yet I've come to see these feelings as opportunities for growth rather than judgement. His ability to remain grounded during his own challenges has taught me that self-mastery isn't about never making mistakes – it's about how you respond and stay true to your values even in adversity.

Another key aspect of Michael's mentoring is his capacity to hold space. Whether I have been feeling expansive or resistant, he has always met me with the same level of love and acceptance, allowing me to come to my own realisations in my own time. This approach has been instrumental in empowering me to take full ownership of my journey. Michael never tries to take control or direct my choices; instead, he offers wisdom, guidance, and unwavering presence, trusting that I will find my way.

Reflecting on these years of mentoring, I am profoundly grateful for the foundation of self-mastery that Michael has helped me build. His constancy and wisdom continue to support me as I navigate my path, encouraging me to grow with greater awareness, resilience, and trust in myself.

Conclusion: A Journey of Transformation and Self-Mastery

As I reflect on my nearly two decades with Michael, I am struck by the depth and breadth of the transformation he has catalysed in my life. What began with a simple moment of recognition – stopping in my tracks to watch his video that quiet night – has evolved into one of the most profound and challenging experiences of my life. This journey has not been linear; it has been filled with steps forward, stumbles backward, and moments of doubt. But through it all, Michael's unwavering presence, his consistent self-mastery, and his ability to guide with both subtlety and wisdom have illuminated my path toward self-discovery and evolution.

What I've come to realise is that this journey was never about following a teacher or adopting a set of beliefs. Michael doesn't offer a road map or a set of rules; instead, he creates the conditions for me to uncover the truth. He guides me, not by giving me answers, but by holding up a mirror to my own patterns and behaviours and showing me my potential. His ability to reflect without judgement or interference allows me to take ownership of life in a way that I hadn't before. Michael has been the catalyst, but the choices and transformations have always been mine to make.

Looking back, a few lessons from this journey stand out as particularly significant. First and foremost, I have learned that true self-mastery isn't about perfection or avoiding mistakes – it's about how you respond to the challenges life presents, serving and doing what needs to be done. Michael has demonstrated this time and time again. His ability to remain grounded in love and awareness, even amidst chaos or uncertainty, has shown me that self-mastery is about consistency, not flawlessness. Watching him embody this has inspired me to cultivate that same steadiness within myself.

Second, I've learned the importance of balancing the masculine and feminine energies within myself. Michael's embodiment of both energies, with such grace and ease, has forced me to confront my own imbalances and judgements. His presence has been a constant reminder of what's possible when we integrate both aspects of ourselves. Through his reflection, I am continuing to refine my masculine expression and learning to embrace and integrate the feminine in a way that feels authentic and aligned.

Finally, I've come to understand that self-mastery is an ongoing process. There is no endpoint, no final destination where everything is resolved. It's a journey of continual refinement – of peeling back the layers of conditioning and uncovering deeper truths about who I am and how I move through the world. Michael has walked this path alongside me, by offering guidance when needed and stepping back when I needed to find my own footing. His ability to give space has been just as important as his moments of direction.

As I move forward, I carry these lessons with me, knowing that the work is far from over. But I also know that, thanks to Michael's guidance, I am more equipped than ever to face whatever comes next. The foundation of self-mastery that he has helped me build will continue to support my growth as I navigate the challenges and opportunities that lie ahead.

This chapter of my life, shaped by Michael's presence, has been one of the most transformative and enlightening experiences I have known. His role in this transformation has been profound – not just by guiding me through my deepest fears and resistances, but by allowing me to see myself more clearly, with greater self-awareness, clarity, and purpose. For that, I am deeply grateful.

While this journey has been intensely personal, it has also been part of something much larger. The lessons I've learned, the growth I've experienced, and the transformations I've undergone are not just my own – they are brush strokes in the larger portrait of Michael and the work he does. My story is but one of many, each contributing to a broader understanding of who Michael is and the impact he has on those who walk alongside him.

In the end, this is not just a story about me. It's a story about what is possible when you open yourself to transformation, when you are willing to confront yourself, and when you are supported by a mentor who embodies the very principles you are striving to integrate. Michael is that mentor for me, and the lessons I've learned from him will continue to shape me for many years to come.

STORY NINE

~~~

I first met Michael in 2008 through a friend of mine. I was living in New Zealand at the time and had come over to visit her in Perth. She knew that I had experienced some spiritual abuse in a group I had been involved with a few years before. Because of this experience, I wanted nothing to do with spiritual groups again – I was going to find my own way.

However, I was concerned that the person I had suffered under was still out there, possibly harming other people. I knew that if I tried to do anything about their abuse, my energy would just be used to fuel their fire. So, my friend suggested that perhaps Michael could help me. It was worth a try, but I definitely was not signing up for his group. Because of my past experiences, groups still felt dangerous to me. I loved the spiritual path, but I felt very let down and disheartened by my past experiences.

When first I met Michael, he was sitting in his office with his wife, opening a delivery of antique knives and guns. His office was strewn with pieces of guitars he was building, motorcycle equipment and electronics – some of the things he loves. He looked like a typical Aussie bloke, not at all what you would expect for a spiritual teacher. He road motorcycles and loved collecting antique guns. Being from the USA, I did not like guns. I saw motorcycles as being dangerous, and I liked order. So, by all accounts I should not have liked Michael.

Michael was not trying to impress me; he was just being himself in his natural environment, wearing shorts and thongs. No show, no ceremony, and none of the false pride you so often see in spiritual teachers.

When meeting him, I could tell there was something different about him, but at the time I could not put my finger on what it was. I felt safe with him. He listened to my story and apologised, on behalf of, for what had happened to me. That apology was so meaningful to me, though at the time I did not understand why. He told me that he would look into the issue for me and that he would see what he could do. For some reason, I had complete faith that he would, even though I had only just met him.

During that meeting he told me that I would be moving soon. I did not believe him, as I lived in the most beautiful place in New Zealand. Perhaps he meant that I would just be finding a new house in New Zealand? He also told me that my life would change. He told me that he did not expect me to trust him but suggested that I work with my friend who I did trust. He never pushed me or tried to sell anything to me. He was just himself, and he let his unconditional love speak for itself.

It was not until later that I realised that was why I trusted him. Everything he predicted for me came true, though none of it in the way that I expected. Later (after I had become a student), Michael showed me through a dream how he had dealt with the person who had abused me. It was such a genius solution, one which respected the free will of everyone involved, but which was strong and life-affirming; honouring, protecting and nurturing the love and the free will of all of those who had been, and who perhaps would be, abused by this person. He stepped in, on behalf of love, and in absolute calm assurance, he energetically proclaimed, 'no more'. Simple and, with love on his side, bound to succeed. And I knew, in my dream, that he had resolve the issue.

Later, after working with Michael and learning what love really was, I realised what was different about him and what I had noticed but not been able to describe during that first visit: he had no judgement. This is so rare. He did not judge me or what had happened. I was certainly judging him, but he did not react to this. He just allowed me to have my experience and make up my own mind about whether or not I was going to trust him. He just held me in unconditional love. His apology had meant so much because if was from his heart. He was addressing me with compassion – seeing the whole situation. He also saw me; I mean he really saw me like I had never been seen before.

While I was in Australia, I met many of Michael's students. They were all getting ready to participate in a retreat that Michael was facilitating. A retreat sounded like a great thing to me, a way to work on myself and have a break from my work. But I still did not want to join a group. I went back to New Zealand but kept thinking about wanting to attend a retreat. I talked to my friend about when I could attend a retreat and found out that I had to be a student before this was possible. It took me a while to make up my mind. The pull was so strong.

I reluctantly started listening to a discourse of Michael's which had been recorded to a CD, and working with my friend. At first, we had to listen to the CD together over the phone, as mine did not arrive in the mail for a while. All of my resistance to spiritual groups was manifesting, but I kept at it as I felt that I needed to be at one of these retreats.

Michael had recorded these CDs from classes, and they were full of information to ponder on. I found that the CD I was working with included so much information which really spoke to the mystical part of myself. Michael has a way of explaining things in simple terms that are easy to understand. He does not make things difficult or unobtainable. It was clear that he wanted people to grow and learn.

I eventually attended my first retreat in 2009 and really had my mind blow. I had the illusion that I was a pretty grounded person. I lived in nature, walked barefoot on the beach, and swam with dolphins. Michael ran us through grounding exercises where he helped us to really sink into the core of the planet. He helped us to have realisations through visualisation and by sharing his energy. By the third day, I felt so heavy that I could not raise out of my seat. I almost missed lunch as I did not feel that I could stand up.

For the first time in my life, I was finally present. I was having the experience of how it feels to actually be grounded, pulled all the way through myself and into the earth. Because I had been absent from my body for so long, the pressure and the heaviness felt immense and I was going to have to learn how to navigate life from within my body, instead of dictating and directing from outside of my body. Through consistent presence, we can adapt to how it feels to be here, but for now, I was experiencing the impact of my neglect, and it would take some deep self-love and self-nurture to keep my body moving.

One of the important things that Michael teaches is that we must be here now, in this moment. This is the only moment we have. He teaches that the change needs to happen here, on planet earth, rather than on some higher dimensional plane. So, we need to be grounded in order for the change to anchor and actualise through us. This is something that I am still working with. I learned a lot during that first retreat, and I am still learning and improving to this day.

I was excited to attend a retreat because I had been told that there was no talking about your outside life during retreat. We worked on staying in the present. No idle chit chat or gossip, just full occupation of the current moment. This excited me because, for once, no one would know that I was a doctor. I had a lot of experience of people treating me differently or having expectations when they found out what I did for a living. So, I was excited to be with a group of people who would meet me for the first time without this knowledge.

Michael, it turns out, had other plans and, on the very first day, announced to the whole group that I was a doctor. I was bewildered. Why would he do that?

I was hoping for a different experience and, despite what I thought would happen when people found out that I was a doctor, a new experience is exactly what I got. Through stories, reflection and humour, Michael showed me my own judgements and biases about doctors and, most importantly, he helped me to acknowledge how I really felt about myself as a doctor.

He helped me to unravel a lot of biases and judgements that I carried; biases and judgements which, I discovered, were causing me to manifest the "bad" experiences I'd had with people in the past. The universe, it turns out, is benevolent, and she is always working through life to reflect our own internal beliefs, judgements and expectations back to us so that we can transcend them. My past experiences were more to do with me and my own judgements than anyone else's. By acknowledging and transcending my judgements, I was now freeing myself up to have the new experience that I had hoped for.

During the retreat, Michael used a lot of examples about medicine. I wondered how an engineer knew so much about medicine. What he was sharing really resonated with me.

Once I had been his student for several years, I realised that he could speak with authority on many subjects. He did not speak from what his brain knew, but rather opened himself up to universal knowing, allowing the collective knowledge to flow through him. It was pretty amazing to witness that he can do this.

Michael spent time talking about the four-body system (the physical, emotional, mental and soul bodies). There were people at the retreat from all walks of lives, and he was appealing to all of us at the same time. Through drawing pictures, he showed us how we can develop one body and ignore the others. The pictures were really funny. Through this, I realised I had been developing my mental body way too much, and that I had been leaving my emotional body languishing. Michael told us that we should have all four bodies developed equally, and that we should let the soul body inform the other three bodies. This has helped me so much over the years. I am no longer a head on a stick, and I now use my heart to lead.

Another thing I realised during that retreat was that, for my whole life, I had felt like I had to give something in order to get love. The love that I knew was conditional love. Michael showed us what unconditional love is – love given freely, without strings attached. This kind of love is so rare in this world.

With this realisation, I could also see that I was getting a lot of my self-esteem from my work. I was not really loving myself. I had no boundaries, and I was taking the stress of work home with me every night. I was a classic people pleaser. This was affecting my health both physically and mentally. A lot had to change in my life. None of this had ever been revealed to me in the other spiritual groups that I had attended. Michael's grounded approach was refreshing revealing. I felt like I had something tangible, real and measurable that I could work with.

I learned about energy hygiene, and this really changed my life. As a doctor, I am exposed to people all day. Because of my people pleasing, I was taking on other people's emotions for them. Using Michael's energy hygiene techniques, I learned, with time, how to be compassionate without taking on my patient's emotions. I was able to do a full day's work with patients and not be exhausted or feel drained by the end, and I noticed that my patients became more receptive to me – they were more open to feedback, insight, and taking responsibility for their own experiences. A win-win.

It used to take 45 minutes to drive home, and I would need this whole car ride to unwind from my day. I used to work hard for a period of time, and then I'd take a vacation to recharge my batteries. With energy hygiene, I left the office and was able to go teach a class after work. I no longer burned myself out and then had to recharge with time away. I could hold boundaries even in a busy emergency room. I was so excited about the results I got from proper energy hygiene that I wanted to teach all health care professionals how to do it. I'm still working on that one.

During my first retreat, I realised that I needed to move to Perth and work with Michael. I had never expected to leave New Zealand, but what he was teaching and the opportunities that I sensed made it a choiceless choice – it was worth leaving a life in paradise for my new home in the desert.

Anyone who knows me would realise that this was a big change for me, as I loved the sea and my life in New Zealand. I had a great job in a little clinic that looked over the ocean, and I had a great group of friends. But I could not deny what my heart was telling me. I needed to come home – to my real home. What Michael offered felt like the real deal. There were no games, he upheld and enforced unparalleled ethics and standards for psychological clarity, and he offered great teaching with humour thrown in for good measure.

He never once told me I needed to move to Perth; Michael only ever encourages us to follow our own knowing, and then does what he can to support us as we do so.

Due to my past experience with spiritual groups, the ethics that Michael upholds were really important to me. I needed to be able to trust him. I did not want to put my heart into something again, only to then find out it was rotten at the core. Nor did I want to be used for my money or my position. Michael not only had a great code of ethics, but he and all of his organisation upheld them as well. The ethics were not just for show; they were lived each day.

Michael personally holds himself to the highest level of ethics. It is not one standard for his students and a different one for himself. In fact, he expects himself to hold the highest ethics of anyone.

Later, I was able to sit on the ethics committee and I saw how complaints were dealt with fairly. All the relevant information was obtained, people could speak for themselves, and then a community made a decision on what needed to be done, based on the circumstances, the evidence, the motivations, and the highest outcomes for all who were involved, including the organisation at large. Michael would offer his input, but it was up to the ethics committee to make the final decision.

After that first retreat, I went back to New Zealand and resigned from my job. I kept attending retreats in Perth until I had finished out my contract. With each retreat, I learned more. Michael taught with stories, humour and continued unconditional love. His guidance helped my self-esteem to grow.

Michael teaches us about the pillars of self-esteem – about how our self-esteem needs to be built on a firm foundation, just like you would when building a house. As we grow, those foundations need to be constantly rebuilt to support our new growth. My ability to hold boundaries continued to strengthen, and my understanding of what love was and was not, continued to change.

My move to Perth in the middle of 2010 was not seamless. I had a job lined up, but my licensing got stuck in paperwork. The organisation that did the medical licence changed halfway through the process. The house I was moving into was sold, and the new owner refused to keep renting it to me. I arrived to find no job and no house.

But what I did have was weekly in-person classes with Michael. Each week, we gained another pearl of wisdom from him. I camped and slept on people's floors until my license was cleared and I could start working. It was worth it, even if just to get to attend those classes.

For the first few years, I went to every retreat I could. Each retreat enhanced my growth.

My job finally came through in January of 2011, and I moved out to the Western Australian Wheatbelt. It was hot and dry, and only then did I even consider that perhaps I could have made a mistake by moving to Perth. Then, whenever I needed it most, I would drive back down to the coast to attend class. A good dad joke from Michael would always lift my spirits.

At that time, I was working in an Aboriginal clinic in the Wheatbelt. I had spent most of my career working with indigenous people.

Over time, Michael helped me to see some of the flaws in why I was drawn to my work. Some of my motivation was my people pleasing and my attempts to satisfy the part of me that wanted to save and rescue people. Some of my motivation was that I was getting my self-worth from my work. And some of my motivation was residue from a past life which left me feeling like I needed to – like I owed something. Michael helped me to start to heal my self-worth, to strengthen my boundaries, and to forgive myself.

After being in Perth for a year, Michael encouraged me to really embrace my potential and take a leap of faith. One of the things I admired about Michael was that he put himself fully into any project he felt called to. He gave it all of him. If the project failed, he would let himself feel how that felt, but he never wasted time feeling sorry for himself or behaving like a victim. He just found the next thing that he needed to put his energy into.

I felt to follow his lead and take an empty-handed leap into the void. I had training as a holistic doctor and had always wanted to work in an integrated clinic. I had no business training, but I felt the draw to open that integrated clinic I had always dreamed of. With Michael's guidance, this came to fruition. He never told me what to do – he just encouraged me to follow my dreams.

I am so thankful that my friend suggested that I meet Michael all those years ago. I am glad that I overcame my fear of groups and started to work with him. I know that I am a better doctor for this. Now, I can hold my patients in empathy and compassion. I do not gleam my self-esteem from my patients' outcomes. I use my energy hygiene all the time. I also know that I am a better person for working with Michael. I now love myself and value myself. I show up in the world as a whole person. I am so grateful. And I even love living in the desert.

STORY TEN

~~~

Words feel wholly inadequate for capturing the fullness of the experiences I've had with Michael, as the most significant of them occur on wordless levels – an energetic resonance process where Michael "shows us" a huge breadth and depth of love, wisdom and greater truths in a myriad of expressions. In this, coupled with working with Michael over many years, change happens gradually and is profoundly integrated over time, so it's difficult to remember how we were before or to fully quantify quite how we've changed through the mentoring relationship with Michael.

It's also true that we only see as much of Michael (and what he invites us to partake of) as we are open, ready and willing for. Reflecting on the journey and writing this chapter highlights my own limitations, and through all of this I have attempted to convey here some of my memorable impressions of working with Michael.

I first encountered Michael on the CD recording of a class he facilitated on the topic of worthiness. I had been drawn to personal development and healing for some time, as a result of painful, lonely and isolating childhood experiences. I had read so many self-help books, gathering a wealth of theoretical information, but it was making no material difference to my life as I had scant connection with myself or how I was actually feeling. Unbeknownst to me I was starved for real love and self-esteem, the kind that deeply nourishes and enables human and spiritual growth from within.

Listening to Michael was an unusual and surprising experience which I didn't fully understand at the time. His discourse wasn't as full of fascinating theories as my self-help books, yet despite myself I found I was drawn to keep returning to the recording, listening to it again each day. The energetic attraction went beyond my thinking mind; there was a strength, steadiness, truth and such a familiar reassurance to Michael's energy. As I soaked up the lecture, his energy felt tangible, somehow infectious and transformative at the level of my very being – a sort of tuning fork experience that opened me to a feeling of worthiness at my core, rather than just an idea of it in my head.

Over the ensuing months, this initial experience was followed by listening to more of Michael's recorded discourses on various aspects of the spiritual process – always bamboozling my mind while opening me to subtler feeling experiences.

By the time I met Michael in the flesh a year and a half later, it was like meeting a dear and familiar friend – in part from listening to his recorded discourses and also, as I was gradually to discover, from shared soul experiences together over time.

Like many of us, my formative years had been lacking in truly unconditional love. I was more accustomed to various forms of conditional love as well as energetic and psychological games masquerading as love; I had grown up in fairly constant fear of rejection and attack, becoming conditioned by an atmosphere of guilt and shame if I didn't mould myself to others' expectations.

Needless to say, I didn't know what healthy, love-based boundaries were, not having had these modelled or held for me. This has continued to be a vast area of ongoing learning with Michael through the years. It takes time and effort to undo the old programming, yet there is a simplicity, depth and directness available in working on this alchemically with Michael, and I have marvelled at how this is so much more accelerated, unexpected and magical than what I've achieved through sitting in any therapist's chair.

I remember one particular incident when I cracked a joke in class, Michael turned to me and said very seriously, 'Is that supposed to be funny?'. A huge chasm of suppressed childhood shame and embarrassment erupted for me, with deep feeling memories of harsh parental criticism in public. I wished the proverbial ground would open and swallow me up. I sat there in the class with my eyes closed, just breathing and feeling my way through the intensity of emotions welling up, bringing acceptance to myself as I had been taught to do through the Cosmosis® teachings.

As the minutes unfolded, it gradually dawned on me that there was no criticism or attack underway and I was actually held in the strongest space of the most compassionate love. I had a sense that it was all okay and that I was safe.

Michael was chatting away to the students on various topics, and all the while I was in this wonderful, healing, transformative space. I gratefully took the opportunity to feel and heal the shame and pain as deeply as I could access it, and I felt quite different for allowing this catharsis to unfold.

The following day, in my sense of wonder at the whole process, I asked Michael if we couldn't just work like this every day and so clear through all the emotional baggage super-efficiently. He, of course, shared with me that these things can only happen when the opportunity and timing is "right" and the student is an open and willing participant.

I have always found Michael to have a remarkable ability to seize and maximise these opportunities for the learning, healing, growth and betterment of those around him, even in some unconventional moments and times of deep personal significance, including at his own mother's funeral when he shared some of her life story with us for our benefit. I have been moved and inspired by his willingness to put the service of love and the highest good at the forefront in this way, no matter the circumstances, and even in this particular situation where most people would be focussed solely on their own personal loss rather than the collective healing and upliftment opportunity which was available.

And so, continuing on the theme of parents, children and families, I've learnt some important lessons about healthy relating from Michael. I remember, one time, visiting Michael and his wife, Segolene, with another student and her young daughter. It was clear that the daughter had quite a strong personality- she was used to wearing her mother down to get her own way, and her mother struggled to establish appropriate discipline and boundaries. The two of them became engaged in a battle of wills over the daughter's demanding behaviour, and a tantrum was brewing.

In this moment, Michael addressed the daughter directly and calmly, telling her that she could drop this behaviour and simply communicate honestly about what was going on for her. It was as though Michael wasn't buying into the manipulative childish game-playing – he had looked beyond it and was talking to the authentic being rather than the personality. The daughter seemed quite shocked that someone had actually seen her and met her. There was a sense of resounding clarity in Michael's communication – not an ounce of judgment, criticism or attack of any kind, just a very compassionate, firm love with clear boundaries in place, and it felt like a spell had been broken. Perhaps this little girl had experienced the truth of what was going on for her by being really seen in this way.

Over the years, I've also had the benefit of witnessing some of Michael's interactions with his own daughter through her different stages of development. I've always been struck by the blend of honesty, respect, deep nurture and protective love held in the relationship, as well as by the gentle guidance which is woven through, enabling her to find her way and grow into herself.

Within this, there is also strong direction when needed. I remember an incident when Michael's daughter, expressing her sadness over a lost friend, was tipping into being maudlin. Michael and Segolene seized the moment and quite firmly guided her through feeling how she felt without sinking into and being engulfed by her fear. To the casual observer this might have seemed unwarranted and perhaps even heavy handed, yet it was clearly a pivotal moment, and it demonstrated to me the fine lines and the high standards required in learning self-mastery from an early age. I could feel how the lack of such a guiding hand and example through my own childhood had led me to habitually make compounded choices of fear, which gravely diminish human and spiritual potential, and which are only now being unravelled for me, through the application of the Cosmosis® teachings.

In Michael's parenting I've seen a complete absence of the shame, disapproval, taboo or talking down to children which can be so prevalent in the world. Instead, all situations are dealt with in age-appropriate ways, and I've seen firsthand how this dispels the risk of irrational "hang ups" forming. This is very different to the experience of so many of us who, as children, were expected to be aware and observant of all sorts of spoken and unspoken rules about what constituted acceptable behaviour, topics of conversation, or perspectives which should or should not be voiced. If we accidentally touched on the sensitive issues or "no go zones" of the adults around us, shame and disapproval could be rained down on us. The impact of this would then often be internalised, still affecting us into adulthood at the level of our self-esteem, our boundaries (or our lack of boundaries), our sense of self within relationships, and our place in the world.

Michael's example as a parent provides much ongoing reflection and opportunity for introspection and review of my own childhood experiences, my relationship with myself, and it provides a kind of blueprint for "re-parenting" self now, as an adult. As a parent and as a teacher, he embodies a balance of masculine protection and discipline with feminine nurture and kindness.

One significant mechanism through which I've felt this "inner child" healing occur is Michael's great capacity for "greeting anew". It's so ingrained in our human psyche to just perceive people as we've always seen them, holding on to both our positive and negative fixed ideas about them and interacting with these static concepts of them rather than the living, breathing person right in front of us. In Michael, I've met someone who does just this – he meets me without expectation, purely in the moment, in unconditional love. It's the most exquisite, unusual feeling that invites a freedom to be completely new and "born again" in the sense of being unencumbered by the baggage of previous encounters.

This space also starkly highlights where *I* am limiting and holding myself hostage to the past, nervously expecting my old mistakes to play out again or expecting others to bear grudges and keep score, even in minor ways.

Michael's clear and unwavering love in these instances provides a safe space and encouragement to acknowledge and release all of this, and to learn to relate in entirely new ways.

For those of us who grew up in particularly dogmatic or controlling religious, cultural or familial settings, our sense of agency and self-determination can also be severely diminished without us even being aware of it. For this, Michael's mentoring presence of holding space and providing such a clarity of reflection fosters a deep reset and course correction. He respects our free will and partners with us in unconditionally "showing" us more of the truth of how we currently are, as well as the available potentials for evolution, which it is then up to us to recognise and proactively choose for ourselves.

In fact, he very rarely tells us directly what to do, and this reminds me of the empowering teaching philosophy that is about "teaching people how to think, not what to think".

At times, I've found this to be immensely confronting, with huge feelings of floundering in uncertainty while undergoing this process, yet it is so deeply worthwhile and absolutely crucial to finding one's inner compass and restoring a sense of sovereignty once more.

Within all that I've shared here, and much more that hasn't been articulated in words, the trajectory of my development has undergone a fundamental change of direction through the connection with Michael over the years – I am certainly a different person than I would otherwise have been, and so the journey still continues to unfold.

I experience it as a very organic and loving review, a healing and a healthy maturing of the physical, emotional, mental and lower soul levels, in order to open the way for more spiritual potential to be grounded, in the service of love and of life itself – as Michael himself demonstrates through his example.

STORY ELEVEN

~ ~ ~

A Journey with Michael

If you seek, truly and selflessly, to enter into realms of higher truth and to receive the wisdom, love and support of your higher bodies, then the most efficient way to do so is through a process which I will term Frequency Matching. If all is energy, and if it is the refinement (or the ascension – the raising up) of the frequency you are resonating at which allows higher frequencies to descend and reside within you, then personal spiritual, psychological and physical development is surely the act of making the lower bodies (by which I mean the bodies resonating at a slower or lower vibration) ready to receive and act as safe host to these more highly vibrating bodies.

How can I dress my experience with Michael in words, and sufficiently convey his absolute brilliance (and I mean brilliance in the truest sense of the word)? Will I be able to adequately describe the magic, alchemy, love, insight, and healing that unfolds when working with Mr Michael King? I'm shaking my head and chuckling slightly because there's just so much wonder and magnificence.

I have never, ever encountered anyone who is close to embodying his level of clarity, love, wisdom, and exquisite demonstration of grounded, integrated, synthesised human beingness and self-mastery. There is zero egoic grandstanding or "it's all about me" within this man – it is quite the contrary. Michael demonstrates a commitment to the service and nurturance of all life in a way that I have not witnessed before. He displays taking the highest and best good of all concerned into account with every step and breath. All of this evokes a deep feeling in my own heart of truth, knowing, awakening, wonder and remembrance, and it is both inspiring and hopeful.

There is zero doubt that for me, the Cosmosis® Mentoring Centre is the place to be.

Let me be very clear here: right from the beginning, Michael most certainly practices what he "preaches". In fact, he doesn't "preach" at all – he just shares what he has done to get to where he is, and what has and has not worked for him along the way. He has often said that a lightworker's job is all about grounding and expressing love in each and every moment. He doesn't just utter these words though. He doesn't just say, 'Mother Father God, thy will not my will be done'. No, He genuinely walks the talk of these things, and the proof is very self-evident.

Michael is very generous and unconditional with his sharing of many, many, many, alchemical tools of transformation. There is a colour and richness to my life that wasn't there prior to encountering Michael and the Mystery School. Things make sense. There is clear purpose and direction. I have found my "why". I have a reason and a drive to live.

This is most certainly something I was looking for from so very young. In so many ways, Michael has helped me discover much more of myself and who I am. He continuously helps me meet my own illusion and unclarity. He helps me see and move through fear and false layers of identity and expression. Michael is continuously reflecting and encouraging me to move into deeper levels of authenticity and acceptance. It is a never-ending journey of self-discovery and expansion, wonderfully encouraged and supported by Michael.

I must say, the experience has indeed been very challenging at times. Of course it has. Since when has anything easy ever created real and lasting change? It definitely has not been a blissful walk in the park, or a feel-good-joy-ride kind of journey. I know that any worthwhile achievements in my life have come along through hard work and by overcoming challenge. This most certainly applies with personal and spiritual development, and to working with Michael. He has told us many times that we will get out of it what we put into it, and I find this to be true.

This Man is out of the ordinary to say the least. I have never encountered anyone so seated in themselves, so completely at peace with how and who they are, and seemingly in absolute control and mastery of every and any situation that presents. So out of the way – empty, yet simultaneously so very full. There is such a gentleness, yet no sense of weakness. This man and all that he has done, achieved, attained and now presents, has absolutely changed the trajectory of my life for the better. Truly a world teacher operating in the purest sense.

Without Michael's intercession, I'm sure that I would be dead, in jail, or at best living a very mediocre life in pain and depression, unconscious to the truth which is wishing to be remembered. I would surely still be chasing external highs through material possession, drugs, alcohol, sex, and any other fleeting sensory satisfaction and pleasure that I could get my hands on. All as a desperate attempt to get me out of the conflict, confusion and war within. It was a constant battle for many years, searching and seeking for something and someone. Without Michael I would, no doubt, still be confused about life, frustrated in this feeling of there being so much more, yet not knowing what it was or where to find it.

If Michael's teachings and ways can help me, then they can help you. This is a man who has supported and championed me for what feels like thousands of years. This is a man who sticks to his word like no other I've witnessed, and who has not budged with his unwavering love and support. This is a man who embodies true humility and who is always so present. This is a kind, unshakably gentle yet absolutely powerfully loving man who stands for a world of harmony, unity, unconditional love, peace and wisdom. He is someone who won't take any shit, yet he is never looking for a fight. This is a man who genuinely doesn't care what other people think, and a man who tirelessly works to raise his students and all of life up. Making the world a better and brighter place in all moments seems to be his unshakable commitment.

Michael has said several times over the years that from a very young age he just wanted to help people see in the dark. There is, to me, something very sweet, innocent, pure and real about this. He has certainly made this so, which is not such an easy task on a planet with a humanity which seems to be obsessed with consumption, materialism and the destruction of that which is sacred. This, for me, makes Michael's efforts amongst such resistance, separation and darkness all the more admirable.

A once off diamond and a gift is our teacher, friend, and most masterful guide, Mr Michael King.

Thanks for all, mate.

Saying and Doing Things that Don't Make Sense

Michael used to confuse the hell out of me at times. Not so much nowadays, yet in the beginning he worked in what I thought were mysterious ways. It is very obvious to me now, though, that there is method in the apparent madness. He would often say and do things that simply didn't seem to make sense in the moment (to parts of me, anyway). This would leave me shaking my head, confused like, 'what just happened, and what was that all about? I know that something just happened. I don't exactly know what or why, but it's *definitely* something…'.

As I write this, it is actually quite amusing, and I hope it gives him a chuckle, seeing us all, to varying degrees, scramble in our discomfort of not knowing what the hell he is doing or why he is doing it, yet understanding that something significant is happening, and that it is to do with our personal and spiritual growth.

These experiences come with an absolute unwritten Michael King Guarantee. I have learned that nothing is said or done by accident or without purpose. Inevitably, sometime down the track, in a day, a week, a year or sometimes more, I will have an ah-ha! moment. Eventually, something will click into place, and I will realise just what he was doing or saying, and why. The self-reflection and awareness will land. This takes as long as it takes, yet again there is always something in it for my learning and growth.

For me, all interactions with Michael result in deep insight, more love, realisation, healing, joy, laughter, inspiration, motivation and revelation. These consequences are a given. However, sometimes there may first be a journey through some darkness in order to receive and arrive at these gifts. Don't be fooled into believing that the path to healing, enlightenment and self-mastery is all about bliss and feeling good. I feel that this is one of the biggest misconceptions being touted by the new age movement. It is certainly one that I suffered from early on in the process.

It can just be a look from Michael, a tone he uses, a single word he utters, an action or a non-action, a whole discourse, or it could be some tough love. Without fail,

Michael always helps me to uncover fears and limitations, and he guides me to let go of things that aren't serving me, ultimately always encouraging me to become a better version of myself. These days, I just trust the process and go along with the ride, knowing that it is all leading me to a felt destiny.

Michael ultimately provides a service to help people remember the truth, guiding them as they activate, anchor and actualise their potential in of and for love, in service to all that is. He embodies, teaches and facilitates integrated mastery, and is a great advocate of living an ordinary life in an extraordinary way.

This is the contract that I have signed with him – to help me remember, transform and grow into the best version of myself, so as to longer and better serve. Here, it is all about serving the greater good and the nurturance of all life.

Michael has helped me, and continues to help me, weed out many selfish, vain and self-centred parts of myself. Again, he walks the talk of this and teaches through his example.

Whenever anyone says that they want to be the best they can be, life says, 'Okay then, here is everything that is standing in your way of that'. Then, the baggage and any issues that are limiting you and holding you back will present to be cleared. Michael certainly reflects to me where I am being far less than what I could be.

It is not just a one-way street, though. He also reflects my potential as well as where and how my life could be; 'here is where you are being less than what you really could be, and here is the potential of what it could look like if you put the work in'. It's not always comfortable, yet when is real growth ever without some sort of growing pains? These unusual, out of the ordinary situations with Michael have happened enough times to make me realise just how much more he sees of me than I see of me, and also just how masterfully and lovingly he is bringing my awareness to things that need to be addressed.

There was a period of time where every time I saw him, Michael said hello to me in such a dreary, depressed and apathetic way. At first it shocked me a bit, yet it just kept happening. I thought, 'oh he must be super stretched, tired and only just managing to be getting around, let alone communicating with anyone'. Of course, he was reflecting to me how I actually felt underneath the cheerful and welcoming smile I put on. He was drawing my awareness to the fact that just beyond the surface of my façade was this seemingly never-ending pool of despair. Of course, once I received this lesson, Michael's demeaner towards me changed. The world is our mirror, reflecting back to us our internal reality, and Michael is the clearest mirror I have ever come across. Thank you.

My First Encounter with Michael

I will never forget my initial encounter with Michael. It was my first retreat, and I sat in the front row on the right-hand side. I was looking up at him with no real comprehension of who or what he was, or what was actually going on.

I just knew that after quite a shock awakening five years prior, I had consciously searched high and low for something and someone who I felt that I was meant to meet – my home, my teacher and my tribe. I had been searching for someone who knew what I was seeking to know; someone who embodied God purity and who was the real deal when it came to truth, service and self-mastery; someone who I could actually open up to, truly trusting them with my heart and my healing journey; someone who knew what I was seeking to remember. I ventured down many healing roads and paths which were rich in wonderful experiences, however none of them quite hit the spot as feeling like "the one". Eventually, I stumbled across May Miles. She was like a sister to Michael, and she was head of the student management team. She was my in. I met her at my first spiritual teacher's birthday, and it wasn't long until I had then heard of and joined the group in which Michael was the founder.

Everyone else in that retreat session had their eyes closed. I was just staring at him, and I remember the room being so thick with energy as he talked. From memory, Michael was discoursing on bias and all I could see was what looked like the matrix coding flooding everyone and everything in the room. He congratulated me during that retreat for finding my way there at such a young age. He also gave me a big hug and said that we were old friends. I said that I didn't remember, and he replied, 'you will'. These are very fond memories.

I am not going to go into details here because it is a long story, yet for some context I will share that I ended up leaving the group after about 18 months. Although I had a fire and a yearning for service, I didn't really know what that actually entailed. I was very young and ungrounded – the human part of me was jaded and just couldn't keep up with what the soul wanted to do. I had lots of baggage, and I wasn't integrated enough on the ground, kind of like having a high-performance engine with under par tyres and brakes.

At the time, I felt that I didn't have what was needed to undergo the clearing that was necessary in order to progress on the path. I was very keen yet poorly prepared. I was very much into the new age feel-good-all-the-time thing, and I thought that the spiritual path was meant to be smooth sailing. I had no comprehension of what the ascending descension process actually was, let alone true healing or working mastery. My self-esteem barley existed, which meant that I didn't speak up when I could have, nor did I back myself and my heart's knowing. I wasn't transparent enough about the stuff which was presenting for me at that time. If I had of been honest and exposed more of what I was feeling, then things could have been different.

I have found now that one of the most helpful things in a functioning spiritual group is being able to share openly about anything and everything that I am struggling with. I can then be loved and supported during and through that. If it is exposed, then it can't fester away in the background, eventually playing out at an inappropriate time and ultimately causing harm. In my experience, this honesty really accelerates the process. It's not about other people stepping in and doing it for you, but I have found that it is certainly a helpful healing tool to have the stuff which I heavily judge be loved and witnessed in non-judgment by others. It helps me to find my own unconditional love and acceptance.

I didn't do this at the time, and things got on top of me. I didn't keep up, doubt crept in, and I ended up leaving the group. It has, in the end, worked out well, yet I must say that it was an adventure through absolute hell getting to this place.

It was only when I was "unplugged" from the mystery school that I realised just how much love, support and protection was made available to me via Michael and the group. It was like I dropped down 1000 flights of stairs in a click of the fingers. The magic disappeared and the vibrant colours drained from everything. The sweet sounds of the birds I had grown accustomed to seemed to vanish. It was heavy and dark. The love and brightness that I'd experienced completely vanished over a few months.

I now see the school as this beautiful cocoon we are in – it is completely held and perfectly set up for us to learn, heal, activate, anchor and grow. This doesn't mean that it is easy. There are incredible challenges, but there are also equal amounts of support. We are drip-fed indescribable states of being which are potentially ours to hold in our own right, if we undergo the work and the transformation.

Meth

After leaving the group, I ended up in full blown meth addiction. There was a very destructive part of me that took over and came very close to genuinely destroying me, almost taking me to a point of no return. Part of the experience involved going to jail twice, and also, at a very low point, sleeping on the street. All I had was addiction and a small old backpack with a few clothes. It was a treacherous three years of active addiction, which was followed by four years of cleaning up my mess in the courts.

Ultimately, I came to my senses when I was arrested for a serious drug related home invasion and assault. I realised, in this moment, just how far I had drifted from my true self and from love. Realising the harm I was causing, combined with potentially going to prison for five years in Queensland and three years in Western Australia, was enough to switch me on again. I re-committed to service, to life and to myself. I made a promise to myself and to upstairs to do whatever was required to make amends and to get back on track with the job, which was, and still is, to follow the feeling which is housed in my heart of hearts.

This whole experience actually grounded me and gifted me the qualities that I was missing as a young man when I first landed in Michael's space. Now, I feel far more robust, courageous, real and grateful, and less entitled because of this humbling journey. I am willing and more able to do the actual work that is necessary on this path. I know what an absolute gift it is to be working with Michael, because I've had the experience of being his student and then not. I've felt the difference. As previously mentioned, it was by having this experience of being in the group and then leaving that I deeply realised the gifts on offer. The blessing is clear.

Was this experience absolutely necessary? No. I am certain that there would have been a more graceful way to get myself to where I am today. But, as Michael teaches, I can't change the past. There is no point wasting time looking back with regret. The only thing I have control over is what I choose to do now. And now, I choose to face forwards and to turn all of my experiences into gifts. Rather than being a victim, I choose to be better for having had these experiences. I choose to use my past as fuel for my growth and evolution, and I choose to find ways to pass on what I have learned so that others can have a different experience to me – so that they can gain the wisdom without having to have the lived experience.

I often come back to that turning point in time, being arrested on the side of the road, when I am feeling stretched or fed up. It helps me to put things into perspective and to remember why I am here doing this work. It helps me to remember just how lucky I am, and how much my heart wants to be here doing this work – how much I love being a student of, and learning from, Michael.

It reminds me of something I have heard Michael say – 'every blessing can be turned into a disaster and every disaster can be turned into a blessing'. There's always a better way.

I could feel Michael, even when I was actively using meth. It was like feeling a long-lost and distant home. Deep down, I knew it was where I was meant to be, and that leaving Michael's side was a huge mistake. There was no denying that a big opportunity had been lost. I had left a place of beauty, a place my soul recognised, a place seemingly so far away when in such darkness, yet at the same time only just out of my reach. There was always gentle (and sometimes not so gentle) encouragement and love from Michael, communicating that I was still loved, and that I could get through this and make something of it all. The love is unconditional.

The Cosmosis® Mentoring Centre have a rule that once you leave, you cannot return as a student in this lifetime, except under special circumstances which are assessed by the ethics committee, and which are considered on a case-by-case basis. However, where there is true willingness, love, and a genuine commitment to service, there must be a way, right?

I remember tearing up with such deep and genuine soul-feeling emotion as I sat, finally filling out the application to become a student at the Cosmosis® Mentoring Centre once again, some ten years after that first retreat. It felt like Michael was right there at my shoulder, smiling. The whole thing felt like it had happened in the blink of an eye, yet it also felt like 10,000 years had passed.

There was no guarantee that I would be accepted – in fact, it was made quite clear many times that I wouldn't be accepted back into the programme. However, the experience and feeling in my heart said something different. It was that feeling which kept me going even when everything in me seemed to scream that I should give up and go back to drugs – that I will never make it. I didn't listen to the screams, and I just kept going, because there was a feeling in my heart that said it could be done. Sometimes it was a very distant and dim feeling surrounded by very convincing clouds of darkness, waiting to swallow me whole, yet the feeling was always there, so there was hope.

I arrived at a place where I genuinely just wanted to serve no matter what, regardless of whether I got to serve with Michael or not. The whole journey had genuinely transformed me, and I just wanted to give back and be the best that I could be, no matter where I landed.

So, for as long as there was hope, I was going for it.

Gratefully, my application to re-join was approved. What a moving and unforgettable moment that was. I am home again, and I haven't looked back since.

'I Feel There is a Bit More in it For You'

'I feel there is a bit more in the business for you yet', says Michael. This was not really what I wanted to hear, because I know he is always right.

I just want to teach or mentor or coach or counsel or do anything other than be working in construction. I have been desperate to "get off the tools" since I first got on them. I wasn't consciously choosing a direction when growing up, so a direction was chosen for me. There is nothing easy or light about hardscape landscaping and brick paving. It is hard work from start to finish. I hated the job from day one, yet as much as it felt like I could be doing so much more, I was the one that didn't change and who kept on doing the same thing over and over. There is no one else to blame.

At this time, I really wanted out. I was now qualified as a mentor, life coach and interpersonal facilitator, and I was also a qualified counsellor, so that was always on my mind. Because of business debt and court fines etcetera, it wasn't an option to just abort-ship, however I was searching high and low for something else. My judgement and my desperation were a sign, of course, that I wasn't ready to leave the job yet. I also had a growing crew, and so I was managing more than I was doing the hard work, yet I was still just so over it.

As per usual, there was something in Michael's comment about there still being something in the business for me. A few weeks later, I landed my first high-paying commercial contract. Then, not long after that, I landed my second high-paying commercial contract. Over this period, I managed to pay off my business debt, own my earth working machines and tools outright, put an investment vehicle away in storage, and save away a large sum of money. I ended up with nine employees on the commercial contracts. I was able to be the stable, loving father that I always wanted to be. Though not record breaking, for someone who wasn't long out of meth addiction and who had previously lived on the street with nothing, it was really quite something. There certainly was still something in the business for me.

The business also gave me the time and the resources to help Michael build and landscape our new retreat centre. This made my heart sing. I was so grateful to be in a position, after everything that had happened, to not only be in the group again but to be able to help Michael build his dream centre. I was grateful with every fibre of my being to be helping and giving back. If Michael needed something done at the property, I would be there… and did I mention that I'd be grateful?

For me, it was a dream come true. After so much darkness and after being in such a state of duress and tension for so long, to be serving and having this opportunity was a miracle. I knew it! So many times, it felt like I wasn't meant to survive what I did. And so, however much I may have hated the paving, boy was I glad that I listened and not only built the business, but also kept going with it. I have learned that it is often the quiet whisper that speaks the loudest wisdom.

For me, there was huge learning, expansion and growth on so many levels, which came with managing a bigger team and dealing with commercial contracts and builders. Plus, the money was a different and healing experience for me, bringing me a level of stability and demonstrating to me that I really can turn my life around. I was always in deep humility and thankfulness for these blessings, because I know that everything can be taken away in a second.

It made it all the more satisfying to know that I'd worked really hard to get to this new experience in life. No one else did it for me. I know what it's like to have nothing and to be stealing food and sleeping on the dirt or the hard ground at the back of a church or a library, and so I felt like I had so much and that I was so blessed. At the time, I had a feeling of overflowing richness, gifts and gratitude that would organically spill out and over into my sphere of influence. This was a deeply healing journey.

I'm glad that I didn't just pull out of the business erratically and that I listened to Michael. I'm so thankful that I stuck it out and that I waited, because it was this last phase of the business which ended up being the greatest gift. I am now so grateful for my business, for the paving, for the industry and for everything it has gifted me.

And now, finally, after extracting all of the learning and the wisdom from the experience, I find myself ready to step into my role as a facilitator, a mentor, a life coach and a counsellor. Through this experience, I have learned the importance of looking for and gratefully receiving the lessons that our lives seek to teach us. By learning those lessons, we free ourselves up to start creating different experiences for ourselves.

A Male Role Model

I didn't know it at the time, but growing up, I was desperate for a decent male role model – for someone who knew what it was to be a man, who wasn't scared of life, who could match and meet me, who could see me and discipline me and guide me, and someone who I actually respected. I had lost respect for my father very early on. I just felt that he didn't have what I needed on board, and that he couldn't help me in the way that I truly required. I couldn't wait to get out of home and tried from about eight years old to do so. I could just travel and do chores for my board and food until I found my teacher, right? Perhaps in a different time.

Michael is the example and the teacher I was looking for, and I found him at the age of 24. In regard to being a man, he is a guiding light for me. Of course, the answers and the potential are within me – Michael is always the first to encourage everyone to look within and to not put him on a pedestal – however, being exposed to Michael and this whole other level of integrity, equanimity, unconditional love, leadership, nurturance and powerful love in a man has had, and still has, an incredible impact on me. It is like being around him starts to awaken those qualities in me. It reminds me of myself – a truer, more authentic and sovereign self; a self that has longed to come forth yet has felt stuck and dormant.

He reflects great possibility and potential to me. On the ground, this is probably the main gift that Michael offers me. He can't not rub off on me because he is always in close proximity – such a big energy and influence, always around, always close, and always showing what's possible. It has been a huge battle, understanding myself and what it is to be a man in this day and age. What is my unique expression of masculinity in this world? It was hard to be clear on that when I was being bombarded by such terrible examples of men while growing up.

Michael is so down to earth. He is by far the most evolutionarily advanced human being I have ever met, yet he is also the humblest. There is no negative ego in him. No grandstanding "look at me"-ness. I never see it. He is always in this kind, loving, peaceful state of equanimity. Even when he is obviously under great duress with energy work, he is still loving and deliberate.

His example shows me what a spiritual warrior really looks like. You wouldn't even know it on the surface, or if you met him out on the street. And that's the way it should be, right? He is doing the work for the work's sake. The only thing that counts is grounding and expressing love, and assisting all life on the planet to move into more harmony and unity. No recognition required.

I can't escape myself with Michael around. This I love, because I feel the potential of a very clear and masterful version of me wanting to be here, and I am tracking towards that. He draws a better version of myself out of me. Just being around him encourages something better to come forward. It gives me hope. Yes, it highlights all my fear, insecurity, foolishness, and where I am not being my best – he clearly spotlights the stupid choices that I have made – yet all of this is part of the process. I want to see that which is foolish in me so that I am freed up to transcend it.

His love and his wisdom are always there. If at any moment I stop and tune in, his love and his support are right there, present and available. If I have a question, I can just ask it and feel into Michael's presence, and the answer is always there. He never moves out of love. I see and feel him as this unshakable, solid yet incredibly flexible, gentle and very large point of love, light and life that wholeheartedly wishes the best for all concerned. He demonstrates this in all actions and behaviour. Again, the real deal.

I also deeply appreciate the standard of ethics he holds for himself and the group. There is zero casual sex or secret little alcohol-infused drug parties with orgies going on. He walks the talk of clean, clear, higher living in a very grounded way. Everyone, no matter how long you have been a friend or a student, is held to the same standards. Not all spiritual teachers and groups are like this, which is sad.

It is refreshing to have witnessed him in action. I live on the same property as him, so I know that he is through-and-through living the process.

Thank God he managed to stay awake and forge the path that he has, so that all of us can benefit.

Make Your Ordinary Life Extraordinary

I have heard, in my travels, that the new age of Aquarius is about living an ordinary life in an extraordinary way. If I haven't conveyed this already, then let me say that Michael embodies this absolutely. He interacts with everyone in such a humble, clear and kind way. No one that he meets would know the extent of his self-mastery or who he really is. He is very relatable. There are no fancy robes or secret handshakes, and there are no special titles for himself or his senior students. He is just so down to earth, which, to me, is what makes it so much more inviting.

He loves motor bikes and antique guns, and he gets around in ruggers and thongs during summer. So awesome! Michael loves music and is the lead singer and guitarist in The Love Finders Band. I love that he has taken so much of the taboo and mystery out of ascension and being an initiate. He has demystified so many of the "occult secrets" and made spirituality palatable and understandable to seekers at all levels. It is integrated mastery that he teaches, and from my own research and experience, there doesn't seem to be a lot of that out there.

Watching movies, hearing him laugh, and seeing him interact with his daughter and his wife are heart-warming experiences of a well-integrated initiate, embodied. He has such patience and the ability to communicate deep peace, whilst also not sugarcoating that the planet is in dire straits and needs lightworkers to stand up and switch on, encouraging all who have been called to heed the calling and actually start making a difference.

Michael is always pointing out to his students that what we seek is within – that god and divinity and knowing is housed in our own heart centres. He says that the most important relationship is the one which exists between us and God. Michael never says or hints that you should "bow down to him and give him your power because he is an initiate and God's gift to the earth". In fact, he strongly discourages such disempowering displays of hero-worship.

Instead, Michael shares that 'God is within all that is; God is within me; God within grow strong'. We can become our own source on the planet and our own source to the planet. Everything we need is within us, and although we may need someone who is a few steps ahead of us to guide and show us the way, it isn't about being saved and it isn't about anyone else doing it for us.

What Michael teaches is transformation through self-mastery, which is the process of cultivating psychological clarity and working towards true spiritual sovereignty and leadership in our own right. It's about becoming integrated and balanced. Michael doesn't try to create clones, spawned in his own image. Instead, he encourages us to undergo our own exploration and to discover our unique cosmic origins. 'It's not monkey see monkey do', says Michael. We are encouraged to ground and express the unique expression of God that we are.

And Finally...

Honestly, I just feel so blessed and so grateful that Michael has done what he has done in giving me a second chance and in giving me the time of day. With the path that I took, many spiritual teachers wouldn't. Michael says that he doesn't care about our past – his only interest is in who we are now and in what we are becoming. It is because of his wisdom, his resilience, and his commitment to truth and higher love that I now have this platform to truly heal and rediscover who I am. Again, being around him brings up all my unresolved stuff, yet it is complimented with a richness, a support, and a love that exceeds all expectation. It is healing to say the least, and it gives hope of a better world.

I'm not interested in partying or in sleeping around, and I'm not interested in spirituality just being a recreational hobby. I'm really serious about service and about doing what I can to bring this planet into a state of harmony and unity. Through his love and his example, Michael calls this deeper part of me out of hiding.

I found my teacher and my tribe. It doesn't resonate with everyone and that doesn't matter. The ones that want to be here – the ones who feel the love and see the value – will be here.

Michael is by far my biggest role model and the first man I have actually respected. He is also the first man I have met who I feel has advice and guidance which is worth listening to, aspiring to, and embodying.

Thanks for all.

STORY TWELVE

~ ~ ~

A Journey Learning of the Truth of Unconditional Love

Michael King is an incredible initiate and also an incredibly grounded man. The first time I met Michael I was struck by what a seemingly ordinary man he is, and over the years I have continued to be increasingly impressed with a deeper appreciation of how very normal he is. In fact, Michael is completely without pretence, and relates in such a refreshingly authentic way, that he is actually more "normal" than the average person. There is no game playing, nor any hidden agendas with Michael, and this is an uncommon and beautiful way to relate. It is sadly exceedingly rare to meet someone who is truly authentic and comfortable in themselves.

From my experience, it is also rare to meet a teacher who is truly deeply committed to helping others grow and evolve, without any ego-tripping or strings attached (subconsciously or otherwise). I am not saying all teachers are manipulative or any such accusation, just that most of them lack the clarity to be truly unconditional, and where there is ego investment, there is a lack of true honesty.

Michael certainly does not fit the typical image I would have conjured of a "spiritual teacher", and that is one of the things that makes him so relatable and inspiring. He does not float around speaking in metaphysical riddles and making grandiose claims, and nor does he surround himself with sycophants and devotees. After decades of searching for the truth, I had seen enough of such ones and been repelled. I was starting to lose hope and yet I still knew that I was searching for my teacher, for someone who could see me more fully, with all of my blind spots and my potential, and someone who could help me to grow and be more and make the most of this life.

Finding My Teacher

For context I will share something of my personal journey. My search for meaning and purpose and spiritual growth began quite young in life. I grew up in a Christian family and I was passionate about service and prayer and meaning beyond the cookie-cutter life-plan that seemed to enthral most of my peers. Of course, as a young one, I had no clear sense of what 'service' might be – I just knew that I wanted to make a positive contribution and that the idea of accumulating possessions or power did not satisfy what felt like a higher calling to give back.

I set about having experience and travelling and seeking and searching at quite a young age. I decided to leave home and attend an interdenominational bible college to try to get to the truth of the Christian message – inspired to live a Christed life, this seemed to be a viable plan. I was so enthused to learn the truth of the bible, but apart from one really inspired lecturer who was clearly channelling higher knowing, it was all a bit flat and 3-dimensional. I was becoming increasingly disillusioned and knew that my spirituality was not really fitting into that framework very well. At the same time, I fell prey to some really inappropriate attention from the Dean of Students at the college. As a somewhat naive 17-year-old, I was too young to understand what he was doing, but I knew things felt very "off" and I felt very lost, confused and disheartened.

I returned home and decided to study psychology and explore life through intellectual pursuits, which was helpful and reflective. At this time, I was also very aware that I was short on life-experience and that this would potentially be a limitation in clinical work. Not only did it make sense to "live" a little more, I also just quite naturally became thirsty for life experience. I spent the next two decades traveling, exploring various spiritual teachings along the way, and looking for meaning in romance, music, and nature.

The question of, "how do I serve *also* and create a fulfilling life?", was always there in the background, and never completely resolved by the pursuits of life. I dove into some very tough learnings and heartbreak, I fell into love/infatuation several times, *and* I even married. However, the unresolved self-esteem wounding that I brought to these relationships inevitably got in the way. The ache in my heart could never be filled by other, and I now feel rather badly about ever expecting another to do what was my job all along. The healing of my heart and self-esteem was always my responsibility.

Early in my 30's I chose to become a parent, and this was a deeply considered calling. At that time, parenting was the making of me and was a very clear purpose and reason to examine myself more deeply. At this point, I seriously committed to stepping toward my potential rather than looking for meaning outside of myself. It became very obvious that I needed to apply much more introspection and self-work in order to really give my child a good start in life.

My searching included the decision to return to further post-graduate study in psychology. This was a helpful step at getting more honest with myself, but on some level, I also found that I could hide away from some of my pain by immersing myself in the relative safety of the intellect.

Concurrent to this, I was still searching for my teacher, as I knew there was little likelihood of really seeing my own blind spots without wise and loving assistance.

I had a rather chance conversation where I was asking an acquaintance about the importance of working on my own psychological clarity and she made a very casual comment regarding a mentor she knew. Somehow, I managed to really tune in to that little life whisper and to following up on the contact, which finally led me to find Michael and his work. I was finally ready to find my teacher.

I began to study the teachings which were offered, and I worked with a mentor. I was impressed to find such a clear blend of grounded spirituality and inspirational material. A lot of what I learned was completely congruent with what I knew as a psychologist, but it was also much more than that. I could feel the transformational energy behind the teachings which are multi-dimensional.

After some months of being tentative about New Age teaching, I had discerned enough to know that this really felt authentic. I decided it was time to attend a 10-day retreat and explore the teachings more deeply.

On the first day of retreat, I met Michael and his wife, Segolene, and I had a profound experience in this first meeting. The depth of soul-recognition completely stopped me in my tracks – it was a moment in time when I knew, on some level, that my life was now changed. It was also incredibly quiet and uneventful from the outside, but for me, it was as though time stopped. I had little framework for understanding this phenomenon of meeting Michael for the very first time, but at the same time, I experienced knowing, so completely, that there is a timeless connection of familiarity and similarity. I knew in my heart that I knew Michael, and that I had known Michael before.

The truth has a way like this, a deep resonance, like a big tuning fork that the heart and soul can recognise. Nothing specific was said, there was nothing flashy or fancy, just Michael and Segolene greeting their students and beginning a teaching session.

In the midst of this big heart recognition, Michael was very much aware of and sensitive to where I was at in my journey. Indeed, he is always this way with all that he does, measured and thoughtful in his responses, always clear, and always deeply respectful of others and their free will. In this specific meeting I was a junior student, with a great deal of relational wounding – far more than I realised at the time, as I had much of that pain tucked away in avoidance and denial. My heart was fairly shut down under many "protective" layers. These layers were no longer serving me, and it was time I began the process of dismantling them in order to uncover the truth.

I can see, from this vantage point now, how very masterful Michael has been over the years in quietly supporting me to uncover and work through my wounding around "love" and to free my heart. He really is a being of love, but if he had initially radiated that love in my direction fully, I really would have spun out and run a mile. Michael is so respectful and intuitive that he quite naturally moderates and mediates his expression in all moments, to be mindful of nurturing life and growth and seeking the highest good for all concerned.

At that time, I still held many confusing hurts around "love" and attraction and had been in relationships that were a collision of wounding, quite transactional and certainly not unconditional.

I quietly observed Michael and Segolene as they went about their work and their free moments walking around the gardens. They were both kind and really, in many ways, they were quite a normal couple, apart from the fact that the love and respect between them was clearly that of a high vibrational relationship, the likes of which I had not witnessed before. The way they related as a couple was inspiring to witness. In just their day-to-day normal interactions, I could see and sense that this was authentic, that this is the way love should truly uplift and support both partners. This observation alone began to heal something in my psyche and soul. I was able to begin to recognise a truly higher way of relating which helped me to redefine my understanding of love and healthy relationships.

Learning to Love Self

In the following years, I began recognising Michael on many levels and remembering him having been a close friend, confidante and colleague. I also began to remember a love bond which remained after having been more closely linked with him in other lives. Because of my own history of not having great experiences with men, I initially found this connection incredibly confronting. Here I was feeling enormous fondness for my teacher, but then tripping up on thinking it must be wrong to feel love, and that surely it was not right or that it would upset his wife. This was all an internal battle for me, and something I did not talk about. Even without this being spoken, Michael was of course aware of my awkwardness.

I was in a bit of a one-step-forward, one-step-back phase and stuck in my own funky definitions of love and relationships, and Michael could sense this. I was also at a point where being closed off from such a present and productive source of truly unconditional love was holding me back. The teachings of an initiate are not just about the transference of information – there is also a deep and profound feeling-based component to teaching which allows for insight to occur through energetic exchange – and for me to listen to a discourse with a heart that was guarded and barely open meant that I was missing much of the essence of what was on offer to be conveyed. The soul expresses through the heart, and I very much needed to learn to trust my heart again.

One afternoon after a gathering, I found myself standing with Michael and Segolene. After quietly observing me for a few moments, Michael said to Segolene, in a very matter-of-fact way, 'She feels that she needs your permission to love me and to receive my love.' I was a bit stunned by the frank and accurate way that he cut to the truth. Segolene's response was similarly as non-plussed as Michael's attitude. 'Sure', she said, smiling at me with a warmth and a slightly amused compassion which let me know that she understood - that she'd had this experience with other students in the past. Segolene could also see that I was confused in some lower-level interpretations of love and trapped within my own wounding, and they were both gracious enough to have this brief conversation to free up my more immature and wounded aspects within. Anything within me which was using Segolene as an excuse to keep myself shut off from the love was suddenly thwarted, and I found myself with no further excuses.

I realise now that it is a rather common tendency to confuse love with attraction, because unconditional love is such a rare thing. I knew I was not attracted-to or wanting a relationship with Michael in the romantic way, but I could not understand what I was feeling. There is so much confusion in society today around relationships and love, that most who experience a big heart-based love will tend to draw it into the lower centres and senses, in an attempt to run it through human filters of understanding. Hence, for me, I had a big "this must be wrong" interpretation coming up, which was really keeping me stuck.

The truth is that unconditional love is an activity of the higher centres. It is literally the activity of life itself – pure, intentional, and always seeking to uplift and encourage evolution. It doesn't need to be wrestled with, forced, resisted, or even understood. It simply is.

The love that I was feeling was as natural as the life force which flowed through nature. It wasn't wrong, and it certainly didn't mean anything or require any sentimental expression. Michael and Segolene knew this, but, at that time, I did not.

This simple interaction, lasting less than a few minutes, enabled me to begin see more clearly that pure unconditional love can be exchanged without it being anything to do with sexual energy, and without any weird possessive or insecure feelings. Their willingness to acknowledge my difficulty and reach out in a way that could help free me from some of my own mental blocks here was vital, and generous on their part. My challenge in that moment was so far from their reality of experience, but they could acknowledge my concerns, and bridge that gap with kindness.

Having been around Michael and Segolene for more than a decade now, I can attest that they work to extremely high ethical standards. However, back then, I was still very wary of "love", of closeness, and I was scared of letting myself love for fear that someone might take advantage or that I might lose myself.

I had spent much of my 20's and 30's looking for meaning in fairytales and romantic ideas, with a very limited understanding of love. I now had a chance to let go of all that pain and confusion and to be open to experiencing real heart awakening. I was embarking on a journey of exploration where I could actually return to authenticity, and, in fact, I now had the opportunity to reawaken to love as a pure energy, as a part of being alive and engaging in the dance of life. Not only did I have the opportunity to do this, but I was also in the presence of a teacher who could guide this process without any agenda, with full-sensitivity to the baggage I was carrying, and to allow this to unfold in a manner that was truly a revelation from within.

Even here it is hard to write clearly of the magnitude of love Michael expresses, and does so quite masterfully in a myriad of ways. The first obstacle here is the incredibly limiting conception of love that most of us have. This is understandable since most of what we have been told was "love" was, instead, a rather meagre imitation of real love. We stumble on language here too, and we have so much collective damage from parental "love" and romantic "love" that we all have many filters on the possibility for understanding. This is such a relevant part of my experience in my own growth and learning and as a student of Michael's.

To love and to be loved is a very pure and growthful experience; it is part of the nurturance of all life that is so needed on this planet, for humanity and across all life. It really is a natural part of life-force, and the fact that we tend to resist, squash, judge and misinterpret this is a major hindrance. It seems we have swung from an era of Victorian repression to an era of "free-love" (which became free sex, regardless of love), and we seem to have landed in a place of utter confusion and distorted ideas about what love actually is, what it "means", and how it should be expressed.

I look forward to more of us waking up and having a different experience. The more people begin to experience a true heart opening, the more healing can happen on a planetary level. There is a higher intelligence that comes with unconditional love and heart opening, and I believe that many are seeking and searching this way.

Unconditional Love as a Force

There is much need for more love and light in the world, and this is part of the service of Michael's work and presence as an initiate and a teacher. The more of us that can wake up to our true loving nature, the better for humanity and the planet herself. Those living from the heart will quite spontaneously feel a loving connection to the environment and to each other.

However, we find ourselves quite shrouded in fear much of the time. From my clinical work as a psychologist, I can certainly attest to that. It is also evidenced in the rise of mental health concerns that are well documented across many countries. There is a growing wave of problems unfolding from the collective fears that are largely unchecked.

So many good-hearted people are struggling under a thick fog of fear, which seems to be swamping our collective psyche. Perpetuated by our social structures, so many of us are crippled by fear; fear of rejection; fear that I am not loveable or worthy; fear that if I don't micro-manage with over-control of my environment then bad things will happen; fear that my appearance is not acceptable; fear that I don't have enough money or property… the list is almost endless.

When we are caught up in a cycle of being motivated to push away from and compensate for our fears, then we are really disempowered and, ultimately, this tends to fuel more and more fear.

In terms of human growth and development, this fear-based focus keeps the bulk of humanity stuck in the lower levels of Maslows' pyramid. Even the most affluent and powerful can feel this struggle, because their car or yacht is not the latest model, or their lips are not plump enough, and there is no amount of possession, substance, power, or anything material that will fill the void within where true unconditional self-love is needed.

From the perspective of growth and evolution, our primary opportunity in any lifetime is to grow, to be the best that we can be, and to live to the best of our potential. If we get tangled up in the lower tiers of the pyramid, feeling in constant struggle (real or imagined), and being motivated by survival needs, then we are far less able to move into self-actualisation. In this collective haze of fear, there is much difficulty in making any meaningful advancement.

Maslow spoke of the goal and drive for self-actualisation, and later even updated his own model to acknowledge that the top tier of human potential is that of self-transcendence. The move toward self-transcendent motivation, and to consider beyond the individual self, has been described as a feature that is exhibited by the best among us.

This is certainly what I see in Michael: a loved-based, evolutionary drive for the greatest good, for harmony and health, and a restoration of sacredness and of true mutual respect. Teaching is a big part of this service wherein he can encourage the growth and evolution of his students, who can then also pass on their learnings to other people. To break free from the treadmill of a fear-based life is not only a true gift of great reward, it is also a huge service. In this way, others can also begin to sense and glimpse that there is another way.

The teaching I have encountered with Michael provides a very practical process of compassion to uncover our core fears and challenges, and to release the judgements within that tie us to events and beliefs that no longer serve us. There is the very real opportunity to process through issues and transcend them. There is a process that brings real and lasting change in how I relate to myself, and to life.

I have found that psychological practices can bring a lot of assistance to people, and I have seen many really benefit from what is offered. From the "talking cure" that Freud introduced to the more transcendent truths of Jung, there is much good work in the field of psychology. However, many modalities, including psychology, are limited, and to truly break free from living a reactive life in order to fully live from purpose and to cease repeating patterns, we must relate to ourselves as more than just the physical, emotional, and mental experience of our lives. The teachings of Cosmosis®

provide a clear pathway for soul-level healing that is truly transformational.

Love in Creative Expression

I have had a further deepening of growth and experience in playing music with Michael. I have watched him apply himself to learning the guitar so that he can bring love and teaching and processes through music. The first time I heard him play many years ago, it was not the most technically brilliant playing, but the love brought through the musical expression was so very moving.

I was surprised and incredibly grateful to observe and experience the ways that Michael was able to express an energetic process that could bypass my mental barriers and pierce straight through to my heart. My experience was really quite profound, and I could feel the reverberations through my heart centre, melting some of my defensive layers. I was of course willingly partaking of this; I had been seeking, since our first meeting, to be more open to love, to find my own love and to live from love.

The vibrational healing of music and frequency has been a major contribution to the expression of teaching and transformational energy. I feel very privileged to have observed this process and these skills being refined and mastered by Michael. In recent years, hours of practice and diligent application have brought a technical mastery that has allowed Michael's musical expression to really shine. As a flutist, I have had much joy in playing in a band alongside Michael and observing and experiencing him closely in this context.

I had grown up playing music and had felt a great passion for this expression. I recall a pivotal moment, around the age of thirteen, where I allowed the comments of a critical judge at a local eisteddfod to really shut me down. I had performed, and I felt my heart wide open, bringing love through music, and then the feedback offered was cruel and unprofessional. In that moment, I closed off a part of myself. To close myself off was not the wisest choice, but I have compassion for that young me and the pain she did not know how to heal at that time.

The experience in recent months and years has been that of playing music together with love, joy and mutual respect. It is an incredibly creative way to serve and bring love. Adding to the joy of sharing love with audiences through music is the opportunity afforded me by being so close and open to a source of unconditional love. Spending this time with Michael means that I, too, am transformed by this experience.

Michael is clearly working on many different levels even when performing, but his generous and open heart brings such an intuitive expression. There is a communing that occurs in a musical context which has allowed me to open to an even greater connection with the energy signature of love and transformation, enabling me to learn even more about how to relate in this way to facilitate and accelerate my own growth and learning. I aspire to learn more and more how to share of this with others.

Integrity of Character

Michael's approach to human growth, and to helping his students evolve, is a very grounded and practical approach. Decades of disciplined application to his own evolution enable Michael to see things with great clarity. This is also part of what makes his teaching so clear, practical and authentic, because he has walked the walk and not just talked the talk.

I can honestly say that Michael is constant and consistent in his application to service and love. His self-mastery is always evident, from ordinary tasks to extraordinary ones. Watching him learn to play music has been only one of his expressions, and I see him continuously applying himself to learning, growth, and evolution. I see only integrity, even under trying conditions.

Michael has the ability to read the human psyche with the clarity of an engineer (indeed, Engineering was his first career). Michael perceives the soul journey from a much higher vista and is very generous with his sharing and guidance with those who are earnest. He can see which of our obstacles is most holding us back in any given moment, and will kindly prompt, 'this character flaw is really in the way for you right now' or 'this is something that you really want to address'. The feedback offered is incredible, and the perfect freedom with which he offers it comes from a sincere desire to lift people up to be their best.

Michael cares deeply about his students without getting entangled in their internal narratives and dysfunctional patterns. The master engineer can see from an advanced perspective and, being able to see all the component parts of the whole, he can diagnose what adjustments will yield the most positive outcomes.

Michael's total acceptance and lack of judgement naturally provides a deeply transformational energy. Perhaps a bit of a paradox on the surface, but it is in deep acceptance of "what is", that true change can occur.

At all times, I see Michael operate from kindness and great compassion. I have been astounded to watch as Michael repeatedly works with his students to best facilitate their growth and evolution.

'Do no harm' is a guiding principle that I see demonstrated consistently in Michael's life and work. However, his perspective is from a vista that can consider this maxim from an evolutionary perspective. Hence, Michael will challenge his students, and never pander to egos, because it is neither kind nor loving to do so. Neither will he push people beyond what they are ready to receive. There is always the opportunity to stretch into deeper knowing, but this stretching is always measured and loving.

During my own initial experience of learning to open my heart, I can see how Michael gently stretched and encouraged me, without forcing anything or overwhelming me. His approach successfully revealed more of the truth of my own love, and allowed me to bloom into my own knowing. If Michael had simply showed up without any sensitivity, radiating the fullness of his experience of love, it would not have served my evolution. I was clearly not ready at that time, and Michael, though always nudging me forwards, was sensitive to which approach would be most likely to bring about an outcome of love.

Through all moments, Michael remains patient. He is not attached to any outcome. He does not need me to "get it", he simply places no expectations on me whilst offering me a more loving alternative.

Michael is versatile in his being and expression, and this further enables him to be a blank canvas for the truth. He seems to know exactly what flavour of love is going to reach each student – even in a single discourse, we can each receive different realisations. This constant commitment to the growth of his students is very unique and enables him to bring the truth to them without any judgement. This absence of judgement is not an airy-fairy new age "go with the flow" attitude. Quite the contrary. As a deeply principled person, Michael can unequivocally state that some things are unacceptable behaviour, but this is a statement which is always offered with a complete absence of judgment.

Ethical Practice

I have observed the ways in which Michael guides and instructs his students. I have also watched him make tough decisions to preserve the moral integrity of, and fulfill his duty of care to, this group of students. Michael is aware that we are all learning and growing, and often we are learning by making mistakes. However, the standards he upholds are of an extremely high level. I have witnessed ethical practice in action and observed his commitment to upholding exacting standards with full discernment and without judgement.

There are clear Key Performance Indicators for all students and mentors to uphold and maintain, and where people fall short, there is a system of accountability and teaching and remedial care which is offered as support. However, at the end of the day, Michael will uphold ethics over any form of sentimentality, and there is no tolerance for repeated transgressions, particularly from senior students. Having worked closely with Michael for 13 years now, I am only more impressed by the integrity of the man and the teachings. Michael is always raising the bar on excellence, and he works to an ethical standard that is unparalleled.

Transformation

In addition to the integrity, love and grounded practicality that Michael embodies, there is of course the transformational magic. The skills and abilities of an initiate are clearly present, but never flaunted and really only evident when we have the eyes to see, and the heart feel the truth. In fact, those who might seek to witness miracles or to be impressed by phenomena are probably quite cloaked from noticing the magic.

One of my first memories of experiencing transformational magic with Michael was at my very first retreat. At that time, I was deep in the academic world and very energetically invested in the planes of the mind. I sat in the room on the first day of retreat feeling acutely aware of my busy mind which was racing with all kinds of random thoughts. When Michael came into the room, my head just suddenly got quiet. It was such an obvious shift in my own energy, to have the mental body feeling soothed and settled.

I was so struck by the experience that I mentioned it to my mentor and said, 'I am sure he did something'. My mentor confirmed that, as part of the energetic support for the retreat, Michael had indeed offered this stillness for those of us who wished to take advantage and learn from the experience, demonstrating to us that such a state of being is even possible.

It has since taken me many months to begin to master this skill with myself. But having that feeling experience was so integral in opening my awareness to consider that such a thing is even possible, and that I can aspire to hold it for myself. This completely changed and expanded my experience of myself and my potential.

The energetic magic is never a party trick, it is never art for art's sake, but it is certainly being woven for us to partake in. I have experienced this quiet energy magic many times over the years, often in a similar way – by being shown a new potential so that I have an energy marker to match to, and then working towards engineering this in my own right. Michael will share of his reality, often in unspoken ways, and offer us a window into new potentials that we can then work towards grounding in our own right.

There is a very expansive quality to the teachings Michael offers. As much as he demonstrates grounded practicality, the teaching is quite multidimensional. I have had the experience, on many occasions, of going about life and suddenly having a conversation or a teaching discourse from years ago just finally "land" in my knowing experience. I hear the words – I always do my best to listen because I have immense respect for this teacher – but sometimes, I know I am only grasping one layer of what is being shared. At times, the soil is simply not ready to receive the seed of knowing. Yet that seed always remains somewhere in my experience and awareness, and if I am doing my best to love the truth, to grow and to learn, I find that at some point the understanding can actually take root in my own experience. At that point, I am finally ready to understand something that Michael has been teaching me for days, months or sometimes even years.

The path of self-mastery that Michael offers and embodies is truly transformational. Unlike many teachers, Michael is not collecting devotees or creating dependence – he is raising his students up and training them to become the best that they can be in their own right. This has been, and continues to be, central to my journey of rediscovering love, letting go of what is false, and stepping more toward being in tune with the truth. In the presence of this teacher, I can know myself better. I have been systematically unbecoming all the patterns and coping strategies that I have accumulated, and I have been rediscovering my true love nature. This is what Michael reflects for me and encourages in me.

Michael is certainly a deeply loving being, and I have been nurtured in the presence of his unconditional love. But most powerfully, he has reflected my own love to me. He has enabled me to find more of my true self, and to learn to really love and accept myself. In this way, there is complete autonomy, I am just encouraged to be me, without any dependence on "other" for a fix of love. I am systematically guided to a deeper truth of relating with life and life-source in my own right. The example that Michael offers is an always-present energetic and practical sharing. He gives freely of his reality and experience, and he is masterful in imparting wisdom, but the journey is mine to make.

In the presence of Michael, I am inspired to be more of my full potential, and I am more able to move toward self-transcendence. Simultaneously, I have awareness of all that needs to be cleared and refined within me, and an understanding of how to do so. The limitations that I have placed on myself are revealed in the face of truth, and I have the opportunity to let go of what is false and continue to grow. I can also feel and experience a closer heart beacon to the truth.

In the presence of Michael, I am learning and becoming more able to bring more light and love to the world. This is the most heart-singing and fulfilling experience I have ever known. I am finally more equipped to be in service, in ways I could barely imagine back in those childhood years of searching. In the presence of a teacher-student relationship with Michael, I have the amazing experience of soul-nurturance which comes from being around someone who truly champions me to be the best that I can be in every moment.

STORY THIRTEEN

~~~

I write this chapter to share with you my experience of working with my teacher, Michael king, as an offering to convey but a snippet of the ways in which working with him has transformed my existence. I'm almost certain the words will fall short, yet, if by any chance this sharing awakens even the faintest spark of potential to encourage you to embark on the journey of changing your life, the way that I have changed mine, it will be undoubtedly worth it.

The Clarian Call

I came into Michael King's orbit sometime in early 2021, drawn in by what I can only describe as the deep undercurrents of a knowing within.

I recall vividly the first-time I heard him speak. It was while listening to one of the CDs I had ordered a few weeks prior – it came recommended as part of a free online course I had been undergoing with the Cosmosis® Mentoring Centre. It had finally arrived, so I decided to listen to it that afternoon. I sat, took a deep breath, and pressed play. The CD was a recording of one of Michael's spiritual discourses and the moment that it started, I was immediately moved by the energy; it was as if I'd entered a sacred inner room where time stood still. Michael began to speak. Initially I didn't recognise his voice, it was his energy that was strikingly familiar. I knew I hadn't met him before – at least not in this life – yet there was a type of recognition there.

As his discourse went on, it became obvious that he was different to other teachers I had been exposed to in the past. He lacked even the subtlest sense of self-aggrandisement or self-importance. The topic of the discourse was that of a great remembering for me, which seemed to span out into all directions all at the same time. I found myself fully enmeshed in the experience, intently listening through all the parts of me. It seemed to touch into places I hadn't experienced before, which was somewhat perplexing and wonderous all at the same time. It was my first experience of engaging with a constant flow of higher and more refined energies, and while I wasn't sure of exactly what I had stumbled across, at the deepest level, a part of me knew that it was just the beginning of a much larger journey.

I've since come to interpret this first encounter as a clarion call, the frequency of his note sounding with that of my note, lighting the way home.

What You Are Seeking is Seeking You

Prior to that moment, I was really your typical seeker, seeking a reuniting with the Divine. From as young as I can remember, there was a type of yearning to answer a call within, and it had only gotten louder with time. The truth is that I wasn't sure what I was looking for, though on some level, I knew that I would recognise it when I found it.

There was a plethora of modalities on offer, promising to expand seekers into higher realms and to activate higher light bodies. To me, though, much of what was on offer felt a bit like finding the scattered pieces of a greater picture which yearned to be reunited, but which lacked the glue to bind it all together.

Accessing higher realms came more naturally to me, yet I'd become aware of the significant disconnect between the higher and lower experience. Reflecting back, I didn't come across any other mystery schools that taught integrated ascension as Michael taught it. My soul yearned to evolve and grow, yet on the ground life was messy and full of things that I judged, denied, and struggled to bring harmony to.

From early on I could feel that Michael was different; he was light in spirit, deeply grounded and real, yet he made no claims of being a guru or messiah. He spoke of things just as they were, and while this was somewhat wildly refreshing, being a bit of a spiritual by-passer, parts of me were deeply challenged by this. Michael's energy seemed to not only draw out the love within, but also the less-than-love parts, the wounded and hurt parts. It was as if merely being in his presence, whether that be listening to a CD, watching a video, or during an in-person interaction, was enough to naturally evoke this response in me. It was a type of mirroring that would almost stop you in your tracks and invite you to take an honest, unfiltered look at the reality of how you were bringing yourself to the world.

Michael was less impressed with how much light you thought you could hold or how many chakras you thought you had activated. He was more interested in how much love you embodied, and how much of that love was being expressed in the here and now. To be completely frank, it took some time to be fully receptive to this type of mentoring and mirroring. And to his credit, Michael never tired of the resistance – he just patiently and lovingly stayed.

The truth is that a part of me didn't like being here (as a human on planet earth, that is). Life was messy and painful; it was much nicer blissing out in the higher realms. I had become a serial survivor. I'd learnt to use my gifts (and by "gifts" I mean the unique tendencies and abilities that we each come in with) to get by in the world. For me, one of my gifts was the ability to influence other people, creating a kind of "there is nothing to see here" veil around myself, masking the underlying pain I had experienced.

It may be useful to share a bit about how I arrived at this point and why working with Michael became so helpful.

Spiritualising Matter & Grounding and Expressing Love

Growing up, I experienced various degrees of childhood abuse, mostly at the hands of my father. He had fallen to the grips of alcohol at an early age and my mother, while very loving, was severely depressed. From the age of five I felt the impulse to protect my mother from my father's violence and, as a result, I became the recipient of the violence. Growing up in this environment was a somewhat challenging experience. Being quite sensitive at heart, I developed a type of outer layer that was forged out of the necessity to protect the most inner parts. These coping mechanisms, which had helped me to survive at the time, became limitations later in life. I had various issues, particularly with my sense of belonging and my worthiness, though many of my issues were nicely masked up and hidden away behind my perceived successes in overcoming that adversity. I confirmed and expressed my success through worldly achievements.

Michael taught me the importance of spiritualising matter through the Cosmosis® process. This is the process of systematically refining the human vehicle to make it safe host for spirit. This involves clearing out the vessel, both on the soul and the genetic track, of any wounding and limiting beliefs that have accumulated throughout time, so that the spirit that we are a part of can express here now.

This process presents an opportunity to step all the way into the human experience, ceasing all avoidance and denial and embracing life as it actually is, and this was really where the rubber hit the road, so to speak. Committing to being here now really set the foundations for what would become the true journey.

Through Michael's guidance, generosity and unwavering example, I was able to begin the process of clearing out trauma, grief, limiting beliefs and glass ceilings that had been preventing me from not only coming into my true potential, but grounding and expressing love. It was a process of bringing deep love, compassion and acceptance to self. Learning to soften rather than whip.

One by one, the things that were important to me began to change. Being the top performer at work or having a beautiful home became less important – it was my relationship with myself and my capacity to love that became the priority. I could see that this change in priority didn't lessen my life quality, but instead allowed me to bring myself more fully to my immediate sphere of influence.

I remember Michael sharing, 'I have a body yet I'm not my body, I have a mind yet I'm not my mind, I have emotions yet I'm not my emotions'. He wasn't governed by the 4-body system, which helped me to build the awareness that, while these parts were wondrous parts of me, they were not the parts that wisdom would flow out of. Michael demonstrated that wisdom was accessed on the soul level and above, and that it was my job to bring that wisdom, love and compassion to these parts of me, while simultaneously growing parts up and releasing any parts which no longer served. It was a type of parenting, really.

I found this challenging yet extremely useful, especially when compared to the modalities I had previously explored which had offered to clear out emotional baggage in the body through breath work or through various types of somatic release. When practicing these modalities, I would find that, after the initial release, much of the underlying behaviour was still there and that the thing which I had "released" would inevitably recreate itself. I now understood why Michael never encouraged engaging in such practices. How could they, after all, create lasting change if there was no awareness or changed behaviour?

I've come to realise that this was the descension part of the ascending-descension process that Michael had been both living out of and teaching. Melding spirit with matter. Day by day, month by month, and year by year, I underwent the process of releasing more of what was not really me in order to allow more of what I truly am to land and take up space. With that, my life greatly improved. I became much more compassionate. After all, I had been to the places within myself that I least wanted to go to, and I had been able to bring deep love and acceptance to the parts that I had previously deemed unlovable and which I had rejected. I'm not suggesting that I'm done with this process yet, or that I ever will be – I am merely sharing that engaging in this type of healing has translated into more compassion, love and understanding on the ground.

I had come to appreciate that true spirituality was not about accessing higher realms and ascending into the light, but that it was about spiritualising the human vehicle to ground and express more love, here on planet earth. The goal of spirituality should not be to "get out of here". Spirit is generous, benevolent and uplifting, seeking to ignite and nurture the love and the evolution of all of humanity. So, I realised that the goal of spirituality should be about finding ways to *be* more like spirit – bridging the gap between heaven and earth in order to love, heal and serve here.

And what point was there in channelling higher dimensional states if they were not brought through a clear channel? I recall Michael describing it (and I'm paraphrasing here) as gaining to access the clearest and purest water source and then running that water through muddy pipes. Of course, you will no longer have clear water. The water becomes muddied, corrupted and tainted as it passes through the pipes. The intended message becomes distorted. It became clear that, in order to be a channel for spirit, I would need to address the murkier parts of myself – the parts that needed to be raised up and refined in order to clearly perceive and embody any gnosis which was wanting to land.

I'd come to really know a consistency in Michael, witnessing him walking the talk both publicly and privately. It was a welcomed change to learn from someone who genuinely walked the talk. He held the highest of ethical standards, which is somewhat of a rarity in spiritual groups, and which was a really helpful experience for me after having had questionable experiences with spiritual communities in the past. It was and has continued to be an opportunity to review my own standards. Michael would often say that one of the marks of a true master is what they do when no one is looking, and what they choose when they think that they could get away with anything.

Self-mastery is not a frivolous past-time, it is a way of living. It is an integrated and full-bodied way of being – a fulltime embodiment and demonstration of love rather than a parttime display of unintegrated, unrealistic and unattainable "ideas" of love. Michael lives and breathes what he teaches, and he shows his students how they can do the same.

Energy Awareness and Spiritual Boundaries

I recall that one of the first courses I undertook with the Cosmosis® Mentoring Centre was learning about the intricacies of Energy Hygiene & Psychic Protection. This was a deeply fascinating topic for me. Reflecting back now, I wonder how I got on prior to this point without it. I guess it was my first real taste of what it felt like to take responsibility for myself, not just in words and actions on the ground, but in how I held and conducted my energy. It was a process of becoming aware of what I was doing with my energy in each and every moment, and it was also the beginning of being able to sense what was mine and what belonged to someone else. It was the beginning of being able to discern whether or not I was engaging in, or being influenced by, external thought patterns or the collective maya of the world. This was a new level of sovereignty that I hadn't quite come to appreciate in the past.

Michael seemed to do this naturally. His boundaries were always strong yet loving. This new awareness expanded out into a process of paying attention to my intention in each and every moment. I came to see how much I had been missing, where I was going unconscious throughout the day, and how much I was not taking responsibility for. There was a CD process and a course that I engaged with for 28 days which helped me to really pay attention to my intention and my presence. It helped me to get a sense of the things that I was allowing to influence me and to see what I had been setting in motion, not only through my obvious choices and behaviours, but through my thoughts as well.

Thoughts (or mental activity) are loaded with creative energy. To have an untrained or unmanaged mind is to be haphazardly sending out energy which creates haphazard and apparently random events in our lives. These thoughts can also feed or enable dysfunction in humanity's collective consciousness. Learning about this helped me to understand the nature of cause-and-effect, expanded out and applied at new levels. When I took more responsibility for my energetic output, I really started to see a change in the things that would play out on the ground. I was better able to catch myself when I went unconscious or when I started to project thoughts.

Michael also introduced us to working with inner plane beings and higher energies. Prior to this, I'd had much experience with energies of the astral plane from early childhood. I had learned in my early twenties that I could ask those beings of the lower vibrational planes to go away, yet this felt more like I was slamming the door shut instead of setting a true love-based boundary. I hadn't gotten a handle on setting boundaries at unconditional love and above and protecting my energetic field from a place of love rather than fear. This meant that I wasn't always able to discern what energy I was engaging with. I had begun to see that, as a result of this naivety, I was much more easily influenced by beings of a lower frequency, especially if they were masquerading as higher-dimensional beings. It was Micheal's guidance, which encouraged me to align to frequencies of unconditional love and above, which really helped me with that.

It was a wonderful journey of exploring this and refining the way that I interacted with beings and energy as a whole. It was like finding a missing piece that I didn't know I didn't have. Michael modelled what it looked like to only be open to unconditional love and above, the baseline standard that he lived his life by.

This brings me to loving the truth.

Loving the Truth

Something Michael would always share was, 'if we don't have the truth, we have nothing'. He was always willing to share the hard truths if they would ultimately create an outcome of love, despite any temporary reactions or kick back. This confront, while at times wildly uncomfortable, became perfect in its own way. There was never any judgment in Michael's revelations – just a greater sense of being championed to be better. This really helped to highlight not only my own avoidance and denial, but also the conditional love within me. I began to see various flavours of transactional love throughout my life and where I could refine it. This was a process of learning to reorient towards higher and more refined states of love. Ultimately, Michael was teaching me to be aligned to the highest good of all concerned in each and every given moment.

Although in a constant state of progress, I have come to better love the truth above all things. I can appreciate what 'without the truth, we have nothing' really means. This isn't about cramming what we already know into boxes. Instead, it is about opening to a greater knowing – to new knowing – embracing, as Michael has said, 'what you **know** that you don't know as well as what you **don't know** that you don't know!'

As Michael has often shared, ascension is the systematic unfoldment into the mind of God – it is the process of coming into ever-deeper levels of agreement with God, recognising and embracing new levels of Truth. So yes, indeed, without truth, you have nothing because without truth, you cannot realise God.

A Sacred Space – Cosmosis® Retreats

In November of 2021, I attended my first retreat. The retreat was shared with many others of like mind and heart. We were surrounded by an abundance of nature, and we were held in the company of higher vibrational beings, as well as Michael, his wife Segolene, and Amy, our on-the-ground facilitators.

Stepping onto the property felt like being wrapped in a type of indescribable cocoon, which was an experience of great sacredness and joy. The earth felt enlivened and enloved. It was a great honour to be there, to walk alongside other ones who were on the path, both in the physical realm as well as on the inner. It felt much like a reunion of sorts. I still recall the moment of entering the retreat workshop room and meeting Michael in person for the first time. It was both deeply emotional and exciting, born out of recognition for having gotten to this point, and I felt a great joy for the journey ahead.

I recall him looking out across the room with what I've come to know as his loving gaze, scanning and directing love at each and everybody before beginning his discourse. There was never any judgment – the experience was just that of pure love, something I had seldom come across in the past. The process of being loved by Michael often highlighted the parts within me that needed the love the most. Reflecting back in the now moments, this is something that I have learned to deeply cherish and to be open to.

The processes facilitated throughout this retreat were much beyond any experience I had been able to access in the past. It was an experience of reaching into higher realities coupled with an experience of being on a construction site, as my foundations crumbled, and I got to work rebuilding newer and more reliable ones. Michael had created a transformative space for us to come to, away from our day-to-day lives. It was a sacred space, built specifically for us to be able to gain deeper understandings and insight. It was from a well of deep generosity that Michael shared some of his reality with us, giving us a sense of what was possible if we so chose.

I experienced great shifts throughout my first retreat. In the subsequent year, there were deeper changes on the ground, and I felt yet another pull to reorient my life. This really felt like a process of unbecoming, a wonderous unravelling; all part of taking off layers of myself that were not in alignment with who I really was. It was also the beginning of the process of remembering.

In the following years, I attended as many retreats and workshops as I could. Each time, the grounds again felt enveloped in higher energies; it was another return to an earthly home – a sacred cocoon that I'd come to truly appreciate. The retreats and the workshops offered the opportunity to take a deep dive into myself, and a chance to have a go at harmonising parts that felt stuck in time and unable to open, all in a setting that allowed me to be away from the world and day-to-day living. A true oasis.

It's Not Personal!

Through a series of experiences, I began to truly realise that any ideas of being "special" or separate would need to be transcended. As my motivation for self-improvement became more about making myself fit for service (rather than it just being about individual progression or "me" and "my" experience), I began to truly see that none of it was ever personal – it was all geared towards collective realisation, growth and healing.

As a member of the human race, my own progress opens avenues and carves pathways for others to progress, and my role is to light the way with my example, as best as I can. Although all of my experiences as an individual were valid and, in their own way, sacred, how could evolution just be about one individual? This selfish perspective introduces an ingredient that suffocates the magic which is wanting to be born and expressed in its many flavours.

So much of what Michael had been sharing was beginning to make sense. It is only the negative ego, believing in its unworthiness, that seeks to be separate – that seeks to stand out and to be better than anyone else. This learning brought up deep levels of what I now rightfully call humiliation, whilst also having the experience of being grateful for the new learning and for the potential to be better. This is another deep unbecoming that I am still in process of opening to and refining.

As I begin to wrap up this chapter, I come to what I feel has been the most important learning of all...

Don't Be a Spiritual Miser!

In all the years of working with Michael, he has never asked anything other than this one thing: to simply give back and to be generous with the learning by whatever means we are gifted or blessed. Expressed in his words, 'to bring value to our sphere of influence, and to the planet at large' is the ultimate goal.

Michael never placed any claims on the gnosis he shared, he only expressed his genuine wish that it be lived and passed on in a responsible way. For me, it is a great joy and privilege to give back and to contribute to the work of expressing and grounding more love in whatever way I can, as I continue to receive the gifts of Michael's guidance.

In closing, I feel to leave you with something that Michael shared which really stuck a chord with me and which has helped shape the way that I work with others:

"If a modality is about simply relieving pain, then it is also about ego. Spirit is motivated by the desire to learn through the medium of selfless service. You recognise that the experience of pain is an integral part of the growth process, and you welcome painful feelings with gratitude. If a modality cleverly relieves pain so that people just go back to doing what caused the pain in the first place, then it is self-indulgent. It is not about the body/mind, it is about eternal growth and integration."

Here are some final lessons that Michael has taught me:
- It is through shared values, virtues and vision that this is all made possible.
- Ultimately, if we are here to ground and express more love, we must first embody it.
- Be a LOVE finder and live an ordinary life in an extraordinary way.

It is with much love and gratitude that I get to continue this journey. Thank you to my teachers, seen and unseen, for being a constant and steady light along the path and thank you, especially, to Michael.

May love restore the balance.

Afterword

~~~

And so concludes our written recollections. But far from being over, our journeys with Michael continue.

Being multidimensional and deeply transformational journeys which transcend time and space, the impacts of our experiences with Michael happen now, and then resound and reverberate backwards and forwards through our timelines, impacting, shaping, freeing and altering our experiences in other times and places in the past, and opening up new possibilities for our futures.

As humans, we are changed, and as souls, we are changed – none of us will ever be the same again, and the trajectory of our evolution has been redirected as we commit ourselves to the service and the upliftment of this planet and all her kingdoms.

We are works in progress – evolution is neither a fast nor a linear process – but our hearts are full, our lives are rich with purpose, and the divine discontent which propelled us toward Michael is soothed as we come home to ourselves and progressively awaken to the reality of who and what we really are.

We are but a small representation of the lives that Michael has impacted, and we are, for all intents and purposes, a family. We are aligned to the same goals, motivated by the same desire, we value the same things, and we cheer each other on and raise each other up as we realise, integrate and heal under Michael's guidance.

Evolution is a wondrous and awe-inspiring process of recognition and illumination – a process of reuniting with Truth and unfolding into the mind of God – but we also understand and embrace that evolution takes hard work.

If you truly desire to align to Truth, then you must first recognise, heal, transmute and release everything which is not Truth.

In order for love to reside here, fear must be transcended. In order for light to reside here, darkness must be bravely traversed and illuminated.

We know that the path that we have chosen is a path of the spiritual warrior. It takes great confront, incredible insight, honest self-reflection, and a sturdy self-esteem.

We come up against all kinds of resistance, and Michael provides us with the tools that we require so that we can become stronger, softer, more deeply surrendered, but also more ferocious in our choosing, so that we can succeed.

As dedicated points of transmutation and transformation, we welcome the fear and the pain of our past, and we act as the source of light and love that is required so that we, on behalf of, can heal.

Through our inner work, through our psychological clarity, through our lack of judgement, and through our willingness to go forth and carve new paths, we hope to be examples of what is possible – we hope to play our part in actualising synthesis and self-mastery.

We hope to demonstrate that with the right tools, outlooks, motivations and support, you, too, can heal.

To be a spiritual warrior, you need not be perfect. To help others to heal, the most important thing is to remember that you were once where they are now, and then, through deep compassion, you demonstrate and pass on the way that you healed.

Others do not benefit from your superiority or from your perfection – they cannot aspire to something which is unrealistic or unattainable. Others will feel you and be motivated and inspired by you if you are here, present, real, accepting yourself and the journey that you have been on, and exploring new ways to evolve and to embody the ideal.

We encourage you to remove your head from your own arse, and to become present with the work that needs to be done. The planet and humanity need initiates – they need torchbearers and examples, and they need people who care enough to put in the hard work and serve something which is far greater than themselves.

Place no expectations on yourself, but also remove all self-imposed limitations – do not shoot yourself in the foot before you have already begun.

The universe is benevolent, life champions you and desires that you succeed, and there are ones, like Michael, who can help you to unlock your potential and answer your heart's calling.

Just remember to be guided by your heart and to use discernment. Not everyone is true to their word and, unfortunately, too many so-called "teachers" are defective in themselves and are unable to get out of their own way enough to do anything but exploit their students.

Your heart knows – however confronting the truth may be, it has a resonance which your heart recognises and sings along to. Hear the song of your heart.

Remember that you must start from exactly where you are at, and that no step is too small.

The most important thing is that you are honest with yourself. To pretend to be somewhere that you are not, is to delude and lie to yourself, and no amount of external revelation can penetrate a barrier as dense and resistant as self-delusion.

Enquire within and ask, honestly, that truth be revealed to you. Then, no matter how confronting, accept that truth so that you can work with it.

You cannot change a thing which remains hidden. You have no power = no mastery – over a thing which is mysterious or disguised behind an illusory veil. In fact, a thing which keeps itself a secret, especially to you, has power over you and will inevitably rear its ugly head and cause you (and those you love) great pain.

The first step to healing and self-mastery is turning to face the dysfunction. You must cease the activity of being afraid of your own self. You must choose to be courageous, and you must choose to finally take responsibility for all of your parts and all of your energetic output.

When you are aligned in this way, you earn back the right and the ability to consciously and deliberately create your own reality, rather than being the victim to those parts which you are unconscious to and which strike out, creating their own reality for you to experience.

When you have this level of self-awareness and self-mastery, you are no longer a victim to external phenomena and the whims of other people. You recognise that you are always the creator of your own reality, and you learn how to wield this creative energy with intent and purpose. You choose what you partake of, and you choose what you lend your energy to.

Awareness and acceptance, coupled with a deep presence, are key.

Far from existing as disempowered egos, we are learning, from Michael, how to live and love as empowered souls and spirits, embodied here, on planet earth.

If nothing else, we hope to at least convey to you that you are not alone, and that true practitioners of alchemy and magic, though very rare, do exist.

As we often hear Michael share at the end of a discourse,

"Take my advice and please yourself – after all, I could be a raving psychotic lunatic… but I'm probably not."

So far, our experience is that he most definitely is not. In a world where so many of the insane claim sanity, Michael is true clarity.

What Next?

~ ~ ~

If you are interested in learning more about Michael, you can find out more about him here:

https://michaelking.id.au/

If you are interested in seeking further personal, psychological and spiritual development, you can find out more about the Cosmosis® Mentoring Centre here:

http://mysterychool.au

YouTube: Cosmosis Mentoring Centre

www.ingramcontent.com/pod-product-compliance
Lightning Source LLC
Chambersburg PA
CBHW031953080426
42735CB00007B/382